R.E.M.
File Under Water

THE DEFINITIVE GUIDE TO 12 YEARS OF RECORDINGS AND CONCERTS

RESEARCHED & COMPILED BY
JON STOREY

imaginary BOOKS

First edition 1992
published by Imaginary Books
155 Manchester Road, Hopwood, Heywood,
Lancashire OL10 2HH.

© **Imaginary Books 1992.**

ISBN 1 897787 00 6

**BRITISH LIBRARY
CATALOGUING-IN-PUBLICATION DATA**
A catalogue record for this book is available from the
British Library.

**Printed by
Joseph Ward Ltd
Dewsbury, UK.**

This book is sold subject to the condition that it shall not, by way of trade or otherwise, be lent, re-sold, hired out, or otherwise circulated without the publisher's prior consent in any form or binding or cover other than that in which it is published and without a similar condition including this condition being imposed on the subsequent purchaser.

Front cover photograph by Derek Pringle.

CONTENTS

INTRODUCTION 4

OFFICIAL RELEASES AND PROMOS 7
Commercially issued 7" singles 8
Promotional 7" singles 18
Commercially issued 12" singles 23
Promotional 12" singles 26
Commercially issued albums 28
Interview albums & CDs 33
Radio promotional albums 34
Radio promotional CDs 35
CD singles 36
Promtional CD singles 38
Promotional CD albums 39
Commercially issued CD albums 40
Cassettes 42
Postcard singles 43
REM Tracks on compilation albums 44

GUEST APPEARANCES 47
Peter Buck 49
Michael Stipe 54
Mike Mills 58
Bill Berry 60
Multiple-members/Peter Holsapple 60

BOOTLEGS 65
Bootleg singles 66
Bootleg albums 66
Bootleg flexi-discs 83
Bootleg CDs 84

**LIVE TAPES, GIGS & RECORDING
    SESSIONS** 99

VIDEOS & BOOKS 126

This volume represents the most complete discography/tape-ography of R.E.M. yet published. Covering REM's entire career to date, 1980 to 1992, it includes full details of all commercial releases in the USA, UK, Europe, Australia and elsewhere, in all formats (album, single, 12", compact disc, cassette, video, etc.) with accompanying illustrations.

Also included are all limited edition and promotional releases, radio-only albums, and bootlegs on vinyl and CD, complete with track listings, sound-quality assessments and other comments. All known appearances by members of R.E.M. in collaboration with other artists are extensively documented herein.

To complete the picture, there is an exhaustive annotated list of gigs and tapes (both live soundboard tapes and clandestine audience recordings together with details of unreleased studio recordings, broadcast interviews and demo sessions). Whilst this section of the book cannot hope to be complete - it is surely the most comprehensive listing that can realistically be achieved.

The book is an overhauled and completely updated follow-up to the author's earlier publication "REM: A Few Chords & A Cloud Of Dust". We have made no attempt to recount the history of R.E.M. - this has been admirably documented in Tony Fletcher's book "Remarks" (Omnibus) and, more recently, Marcus Gray's "An REM Companion - It Crawled From The South" (published by Guinness). The latter, whilst including a staggering amount of information about the band and it's activities, lacks any form of discography - hence this volume.

Generally, we offer no criticism of the quality of R.E.M.'s songwriting abilities, political standpoints, dress sense or current hairstyles! There is a place for all of that, but not here; we come not to praise R.E.M., but to catalogue them!

For their invaluable contributions and assistance in the compilation of this book, I am indebted to: Bill Forsyth & Mike Batt of Minus Zero Records, Tim Abbott, Pete Jackson, Jukka Heikkala, Marcus Gray, Helmut Studer, Marty Perez, Eva Hunte, Stuart Batsford, Freak Street Records, Paul Phillips, Hans Van Der Waal, Jan Poulsen, Manuel Rabasse, Alessia Tipa, Nik Hole, D. Elsey, Richard Nash, Bill Allerton.

JON STOREY

A note about the author.

Amongst other things, Jon Storey is the editor and publisher of "Bucketfull Of Brains" magazine and has closely monitored the career of REM over the last decade. He has interviewed the band on several occasions and managed to extract from them two unreleased recordings which were issued as free records with the magazine in 1985 and 1992. In 1990 he compiled and published the ground-breaking discography "REM: A Few Chords & A Cloud Of Dust" (upon which this work is based) under the Total Recall imprint. Having completed this new updating and revamping on behalf of Imaginary Books, he is currently resting... and considering the purchase of a large consignment of Optrex.

For information on Bucketfull Of Brains magazine, please write to: Bucketfull Of Brains, 19 Adela Ave., New Malden, Surrey KT3 6LF, UK.

A collection of just the readily available commercial releases by R.E.M., including, perhaps, foreign picture sleeves and unusual song-couplings, would be an extensive one. Also most desirable are the large number of promotional releases issued by IRS and, more recently, Warner Brothers in their successful campaign to help thrust R.E.M. more boldly into the public eye and ear. Particularly appealing are the IRS 12" promos which, more often than not feature attractive and, perhaps more importantly, unique sleeve designs and graphics. Throw into this plastic melting pot all manner of fan club singles, fragile flexi-discs, special radio airplay albums (containing unreleased live recordings, interviews and the odd demo), one-sided discs and appearances on various artists collections - sometimes featuring songs which are unavailable elsewhere - and you have an extremely large body of work.

Even then the true fanatic will still want to investigate Michael, Peter, Bill and Mike's recorded collaborations with other artists (Messrs. Buck and Stipe have been particularly cavalier in this aspect) - a time consuming and wallet emptying odyssey, but an enjoyable one nonetheless. But, all said and done that's just the "approved" product... and only half the story.

After hearing and enjoying the regular record releases, the R.E.M. devotee is almost inevitably drawn to other recordings which are not intended for public consumption, and enters the realm of the 'dodgy-disc', the 'boot', the 'tape'.

Like fans of other major songwriters and performers of substance and longevity (The Beatles, Stones, Who, Dylan, Springsteen et al.) the determined and persevering R.E.M. collector can unearth a wealth of rare material and live performances denied to the casual punter. Some of these finds will be treasured (who could resist those naive, but charming early songs like "Baby I", "Narrator (Jacques Cousteau)" or "Action"? And what about all those covers, from "I Can't Control Myself" to "California Dreaming" and all points in between) while others, perhaps those artifacts seemingly recorded from the third stall in the gentlemen's cloakroom and sounding like Led Zeppelin under the influence of the elephant-tranquilliser of your choice, will be consigned to the bin or, at best, "filed".

The relative wealth of unreleased original songs in the R.E.M. canon (particularly those numbers emanating from their formative years in the early 1980's) and the band's ongoing, and endearing penchant for performing off-the-wrist cover versions have been a boon to both the bootleggers and tape traders, adding spice to their nefarious activities and acting as a juicy carrot to the committed fan armed with a recording Walkman and a blank C90 or two.

With about 50 illegitimate albums to their credit, R.E.M. have proved to be one of the heaviest bootlegged bands to have emerged in the last decade, a tribute to their long-standing cult appeal and fanatic fan following. When "A Few Chords..." was first published the very first REM bootleg CD, "Standing Room Only" had just broken cover - as of this book there are well over thirty different unauthorised CD titles now in existence (all annotated within).

If you should come across any R.E.M. related release not included in this book, we will be delighted to hear from you. Please note that we are unable, under any circumstances, to provide details of where any bootleg records, CDs or tapes may be bought, sold or exchanged and whilst we have listed these releases, we do not necessarily condone these recordings.

ABBREVIATIONS
The following abreviations are used throughout this book:

AUST	Australia
CAN	Canada
FR	France
GE	Germany
JAP	Japan
NL	The Netherlands
PHIL	The Phillipines
PORT	Portugal
SA	South Africa
UK	United Kingdom
USA	United States Of America

OFFICIAL RELEASES AND PROMOS

All entries are in the following sequence across the page, left to right:
    Song titles
    Record label   Catalogue Number   Country   Date
    NOTE: ■ this symbol, after the catalogue number, indicates that the record was available in a picture or art sleeve

COMMERCIALLY ISSUED 7" SINGLES

Radio Free Europe/Sitting Still
Hib-Tone   HT-0001   ■   USA   7/81
    NOTE: Second pressing has Hib-Tone address on label.

Wolves, Lower (flexi-disc)
Trouser Press   #12   USA   12/82
    NOTE: Other track is "Russian Roulette" by Lords Of The New Church, free with "Trouser Press" magazine Issue 80. The magazine was originally offered an alternate take of "Gardening At Night" but prefered to use the album version of "Wolves, Lower"!!

Radio Free Europe (LP version)/There She Goes Again
IRS   IR-9916   USA   4/83

Radio Free Europe (edited)/There She Goes Again
IRS   IR-9916   ■   USA   4/83

Radio Free Europe/There She Goes Again
IRS   PFP 1017   ■   UK   8/83
Illegal   ILSA 3567   ■   NL   8/83

So. Central Rain (I'm Sorry)/King Of The Road
IRS   IR-9927   ■   USA   5/84
IRS   IR 9927   CAN   /84
IRS   IRS 105   UK   3/84
Illegal   ES 971   AUST   /84
IRS   A 4255   ■   NL   6/84

(Don't Go Back To) Rockville/Wolves, Lower
IRS   IRS 107   ■   UK   6/84
IRS   ILSA 4734   ■   NL   /84
Illegal   ILSA 4734   ■   SPAIN   /84

(Don't Go Back To) Rockville (edited version, 3.51)/Catapult (live)
IRS   IR-9931   ■   USA   8/84
    NOTE: Live cut recorded Seattle, WA, USA 27/6/84.

Tighten Up (one-sided flexi-disc)
Bucketfull Of Brains   BOB.5   UK   3/85

Can't Get There From Here/Bandwagon
IRS   IRS 52642   ■   USA   6/85
IRS   IRM 102   ■   UK   7/85
Illegal   ILSA 6384   ■   SPAIN   /85
IRS   6384   ■   NL   /85
IRS   IRS 52642   ■   CAN   /85

Driver 8/Crazy
IRS   IRS 52678   ■   USA   9/85
    NOTE: "Crazy" remixed by Steve Fjelstad.

Can't Get There From Here/Driver 8
IRS   ES 1082   AUST   /85

Wendell Gee/Crazy
IRS   IRM.105   ■   UK   9/85
IRS   ILSA 6587   ■   NL   9/85

Hib-Tone HT 001

IRS IR-9916

Illegal ILSA 3567

IRS 105

IRS IRS 107

IRS IR 9931

Wendell Gee/Crazy/Ages Of You/Burning Down
☐	IRS	IRMD.105	■	UK	9/85

NOTE: Gatefold double 7" pack.

Wendell Gee/Crazy
☐	IRS	ILSA 6587		NL	9/85

Femme Fatale (flexi-disc)
☐	The Bob	REAL 005		USA	6/86

NOTE: Some copies in red vinyl, some black, some with limited edition picture sleeve

Fall On Me/Rotary Ten
☐	IRS	IRS 52883	■	USA	7/86
☐	IRS	52883	■	CAN	/86
☐	IRS	IRM 121	■	UK	9/86

NOTE: UK issue has unique picture sleeve.

Fall On Me/Rotary Ten
☐	IRS	ILSA 7302	■	NL	9/86
☐	IRS	ES 1170		AUST	/86

Superman/White Tornado
☐	IRS	IRS 52971	■	USA	11/86
☐	IRS	52971	■	CAN	/86
☐	IRS	IRM 128	■	UK	3/87
☐	IRS	650225 7		AUST	/86
☐	IRS	ILS 650 225 7		NL	/86

The One I Love/Maps And Legends (live)
☐	IRS	IRS 53171	■	USA	9/87
☐	IRS	53171	■	CAN	/87

NOTE: Live cut recorded at McCabe's Guitar Shop, San Francisco 24/5/87

It's The End Of The World As We Know It (And I Feel Fine)/This One Goes Out (live)
☐	IRS	IRM 145	■	UK	9/87

NOTE: Live cut recorded at McCabe's Guitar Shop, San Francisco 24/5/87

It's The End Of The World As We Know It (and I Feel Fine)/Last Date
☐	IRS	IRS 651348 7		AUST	/87

The One I Love/Last Date
☐	IRS	IRM 146	■	UK	11/87

The One I Love/Maps And Legends (live)
☐	IRS	ILS 6511137	■	NL	/87
☐	IRS	IRS 6511137	■	AUST	/87
☐	IRS	IRS 204 5377		NL	/87

The One I Love (one-sided disc)
☐	IRS	04SP 1072	■	JAPAN	/87

The One I Love/Maps And Legends
☐	CBS	SSC 6067		SA	/87

It's The End Of The World As We Know It (And I Feel Fine)/Last Date
☐	IRS	IRS 53220	■	USA	1/88
☐	IRS	53220	■	CAN	/88

Finest Worksong/Time After Time Etc.
☐	IRS	IRM 161	■	UK	4/88

Finest Worksong (LP vers)/Time After Time etc(live)
☐	IRS	ILS 651320 7	■	NL	/88

The One I Love/Fall On Me
☐	IRS	IRM 173	■	UK	11/88

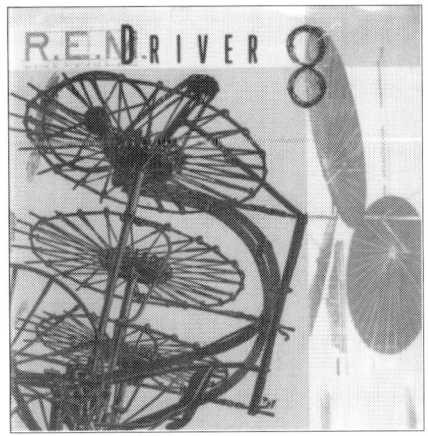
IRS IRS-52678

The Bob flexi-disc REAL 005

IRS IRM 102

IRS ILS A 6384

IRS IRMD.105

IRS ILSA 6587

Orange Crush/Memphis Train Blues
- [ ] Warner Brothers — 7.27652 — ■ — USA☐ — 11/88
- [ ] Warner Brothers — 7.27652 — ■ — AUST — /88

Stand (LP version)/Pop Song 89 (LP version)
- [ ] Warner Brothers — 7-21864 — USA — /88
  NOTE: Warner Bros 'Back To Back Hits' series.

Stand/same
- [ ] Warner Brothers — WB-77-661 — PHIL — /88

Stand/Memphis Train Blues
- [ ] Warner Brothers — 7.27688-7 — ■ — USA — 1/89

Stand/Memphis Train Blues
- [ ] Warner Brothers — W7577X☐ — ■ — UK — 1/89
  NB: in recycled sleeve

Stand/Memphis Train Blues
- [ ] Warner Brothers — W7577 — ■ — UK — 1/89
  NOTE: standard, not recycled, sleeve.

Stand/Memphis Train Blues
- [ ] Warner Brothers — 9.27577.7 — ■ — GE — 1/89

Pop Song 89/Pop Song 89 (acoustic version)
- [ ] Warner Brothers — 7.27640 — ■ — USA — 5/89
- [ ] Warner Brothers — 76407 — CAN — /89

Orange Crush/Ghost Riders
- [ ] Warner Brothers — W2960 — ■ — UK — 5/89
  NOTE: standard, not recycled, sleeve.

Orange Crush/Ghost Riders
- [ ] Warner Brothers — W2960X — ■ — UK — 5/89

Orange Crush/Ghost Riders
- [ ] Warner Brothers — W2960B — ■ — UK — 5/89
  NOTE: Limited edition boxed set including "Ecology" tour poster.

Orange Crush/Memphis Tarin Blues
- [ ] Warner Brothers — 9.27652.7 — ■ — GE — /88

Stand/Pop Song 89 (acoustic version)
- [ ] Warner Brothers — W2833 — ■ — UK — 8/89

Stand/Pop Song 89 (acoustic version)
- [ ] Warner Brothers — ☐W2833W — ■ — UK — 8/89
  NOTE: Special limited edition wrap-over sleeve.

Get Up/Funtime
- [ ] Warner Brothers — 7.22791 — ■ — USA — 10/89
- [ ] Warner Brothers — 27917 — CAN — /89

"Singleactiongreen" (4 x 7" boxed set)
- [ ] Warner Brothers — 9.22780-7 — USA — 11/89
  Including: Orange Crush/Ghost Riders
  Warner Brothers — W2960 — ■ — UK (!) — /89
  Pop Song 89/Pop Song 89 (acoustic)
  Warner Brothers — 7.27640 — ■ — USA
  Get Up/Funtime
  Warner Brothers — 7.22791 — ■ — USA
  Stand/Memphis Train Blues
  Warner Brothers — 7.27688 — ■ — USA
  Note: also includes poster.

Dark Globe (flexi-disc)
- [ ] "Sassy" magazine — (no number) — USA — 1/90

IRS IRM 121

IRS IRS 52883

IRS ILS 650 225 7

IRS IRS 53171

IRS 04SP 1072 - One I Love

IRS IRM 145

IRS IRM 173

IRS IRS 53220

IRS IRM 161

Warner Brothers 9.27652.7

Warner Brothers W2833

Warner Brothers 7.27688-7

Losing My Religion/Rotary Eleven
☐ Warner Brothers   7.19392   USA   /91
☐ Warner Brothers   W0015   ■   UK   2/91
☐ Warner Brothers   W0015   ■   FR   /91

Shiny Happy People/Forty Second Song
☐ Warner Brothers   7.19242   USA   5/91
☐ Warner Brothers   W0027   ■   UK   5/91

Near Wild Heaven/Pop Song 89 (acoustic)
☐ Warner Brothers   W0055   ■   UK   8/91

The One I Love/Crazy
☐ IRS   IRM 178   ■   UK   9/91

The One I Love/Maps & Legends (live)
☐ IRS   IC 006 2045377   GE   /91

Radio Song/Love Is All Around (live)
☐ Warner Brothers   5439-19246-7   GE   11/91
☐ Warner Brothers   W0072   ■   UK   11/91
   NOTE: Live track recorded for 'Rockline' LA 1/4/91

It's The End Of The World As We Know It (And I Feel Fine)/Radio Free Europe (LP version)
☐ IRS   IRM 180   ■   UK   12/91

Losing My Religion/Losing My Religion (live acoustic version)
☐ Warner Brothers   9362-40399-7   ■   GE   /92
   NOTE: 'Song of the year' on cover. Live track recorded for 'Rockline' LA 1/4/91

Academy Fight Song (live)/THE COAL PORTERS Watching Blue Grass Burn
☐ Bucketfull Of Brains   BOB.32   ■   UK   2/92
   NOTE: Given away free with double-issue 39/40 of 'Bucketfull Of Brains' magazine. Live track recorded at The Coliseum, Greensboro, NC, USA, 11/89.

Drive/World Leader Pretend
☐ Warner Brothers   918708-7   ■   GE   9/92

Warner Brothers 7.22791

Warner Brothers W0015

Warner Brothers 9362-40399-7

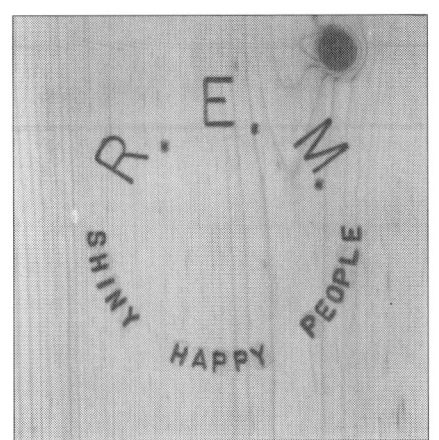
Warner Brothers W0027

Warner Brothers W0055

Warner Brothers W0072

Bucketfull Of Brains BOB.32

Warner Brothers 918708-7

PAGE 16

Photo by Derek Pringle.

PROMOTIONAL & NON-COMMERCIAL 7" RECORDS

	Radio Free Europe (edited)/same			
☐	IRS	IRS 9916	USA	/83
	Radio Free Europe/There She Goes Again			
☐	IRS	PFP 1017 ■	UK	7/83
☐	Illegal	ES 875	AUST	83
	Talk About The Passion/same			
☐	IRS	PFP 1026	UK	11/87
	So. Central Rain (I'm Sorry)/same			
☐	IRS	IR 9927	USA	3/84
	So. Central Rain (I'm Sorry)/King Of The Road			
☐	IRS	IRS 105 ■	UK	3/84
☐	Illegal	ES 971	AUST	/84
	(Don't Go Back To) Rockville/same			
☐	IRS	IRS 9931	USA	/84
☐	IRS	IRS 107 ■	UK	/84
	(Don't Go Back To) Rockville (edited)/same			
☐	IRS	IRS (DJ) 107 ■	UK	/84
	(Don't Go Back To) Rockville (1 sided)			
☐	Illegal	ILSA 4734 ■	SPAIN	/84
	Can't Get There From Here/same			
☐	IRS	IRS 52642 ■	USA	/85
	Can't Get There From Here (1 sided)			
☐	Epic	(no number) ■	SPAIN	/85
	Can't Get There From Here/Driver 8			
☐	IRS	ES 1082	AUST	/85
	Tighten Up (1 sided hard vinyl test pressing)			
☐	Bucketfull Of Brains	(no number)	UK	3/85
	Driver 8/same			
☐	IRS	IRS 52678 ■	USA	9/85
	Wendell Gee (2.56)/BEAT RODEO: Just Friends/Without You			
☐	IRS	IRSP 857	CAN	/85
	Fall On Me/same			
☐	IRS	IRS 52883 ■	USA	8/86
	Superman/same			
☐	IRS	IRS 52971 ■	USA	11/86
	Superman/White Tornado			
☐	IRS	IRS 52971 ■	CAN	/86
	TIMBUK 3: The Future's So Bright, I Gotta Wear Shades/**Superman**			
☐	CBS/Sony	XDSP 93083 ■	JAP	/86
	NOTE: joint promo single, R.E.M. only featured on b-side			
	The One I Love/same			
☐	IRS	IRS 53171 ■	USA	/87
☐	IRS	IRS 53171 ■	CAN	/87
	The One I Love/Maps And Legends (live)			
☐	IRS	ILS 6511137 ■	GE	/87
	NOTE: unique wrap-around sleeve to promote German concert.			

Epic (un-numbered, one-sided disc)

IRS IRS 52971

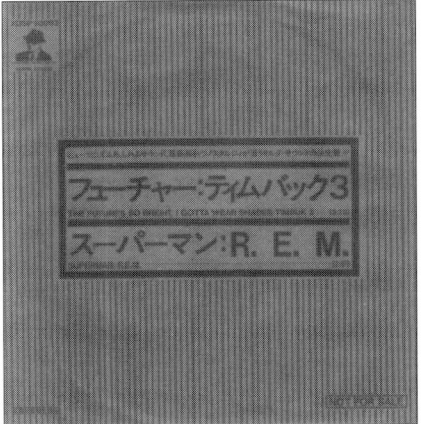
CBS/Sony XDSP 93083

IRS ILS 6511137

IRS IRM 161

Warner Brothers PRO 541

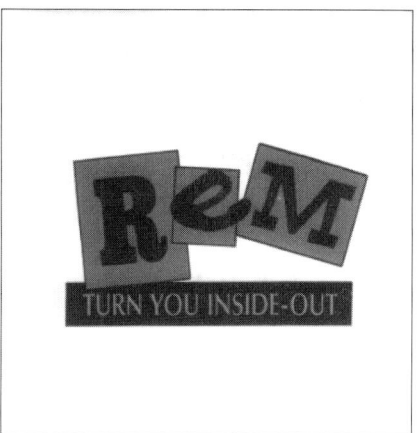

Warner Brothers 1.087

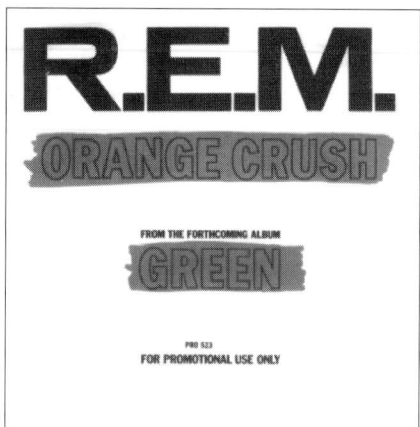

Warner Brothers PRO 523

Warner Brothers 1.008

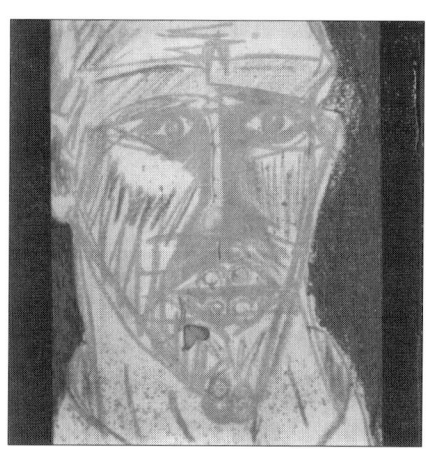

REM Fan Club single 1988

Warner Brothers 1.033

REM Fan Club single 1989

It's The End Of The World As We Know It (And I Feel Fine)/Last Date				
☐ IRS	IRS 53220	■	USA	/87
It's The End Of The World As We Know It (And I Feel Fine)/Last Date				
☐ IRS	IRS 651348 7		AUST	/87
NOTE: white label				
It's The End Of The World As We Know It (And I Feel Fine)/This One Goes Out (Live)				
☐ IRS	IRM 145		UK	9/87
NOTE: Promo copies have A & B labels. Live track recorded at McCabe's Guitar Shop, Santa Monica, Ca, USA 24/5/87				
It's The End Of The World As We Know It (And I Feel Fine)				
NOTE: 1 sided single.				
☐ IRS	ARI 2066	■	SPAIN	/87
Finest Worksong/Time After Time etc (live)				
☐ IRS	IRM 161	■	UK	4/88
NOTE: Promo release same as stock copy but with info sticker on reverse of pic sleeve. Live track recorded at Muziakcentrum, Utrecht, Holland, 14/9/87				
Finest Worksong/Time After Time etc (live)				
☐ IRS	ILS 651320.7	■	NL	/88
Orange Crush/same				
☐ Warner Brothers	PRO-523	■	GE	/88
☐ Warner Brothers	1.008	■	SPAIN	/88
Pop Song 89/Orange Crush				
☐ Warner Brothers	PRO-541	■	GE	/88
Parade Of The Wooden Soldiers/See No Evil				
☐ REM Fan Club	U-23518M	■	USA	12/88
NOTE: Green vinyl. Mailed to fan club members in specially printed envelope.				
Pop Song 89/same				
☐ Warner Brothers	PRO-76407		CAN	/89
Stand/same				
☐ Warner Brothers	7.27688		USA	/89
☐ Warner Brothers	1.033	■	SPAIN	/89
Stand/Memphis Train Blues				
NOTE: : same as commercial release but with information sticker on reverse				
☐ Warner Brothers	W7577	■	UK	1/89
Stand/Pop Song '89 (acoustic version)				
☐ Warner Brothers	W2833	■	UK	8/89
NOTE: same as commercial release but with information sticker on reverse.				
Turn You Inside Out/same				
☐ Warner Brothers	1.087	■	SPAIN	/89
Get Up/same				
☐ Warner Brothers	7-22791	■	USA	/89
Academy Fight Song/Good King Wenceslas				
☐ REM Fan Club	(no number)	■	USA	12/89
NOTE: Mailed to fan club members with folded black & white poster sleeve.				
Ghost Reindeer In The Sky/Summertime				
☐ REM Fan Club	(no number)		USA	12/90
NOTE: white label test pressing.				
☐ REM Fan Club	(no number)	■	USA	12/90
Shiny Happy People/same				
☐ Warner Brothers	1378	■	SPAIN	/91
Losing My Religion (live acoustic version)/same				
☐ Warner Brothers		■	SPAIN	/91

☐	**Near Wild Heaven/Rotary Eleven**				
	Warner Brothers	PRO 607	■	GE	/91
☐	**Baby, Baby/Christmas Griping**				
	REM Fan Club	(no number)	■	USA	11/91
	NOTE: Limited edition of 4,000 copies.				
☐	**It's The End Of The World As We Know It (And I Feel Fine)/same**				
	Hispavox		■	SPAIN	/91
	Academy Fight Song (live)/THE COAL PORTERS Watching Blue Grass Burn				
	NOTE: white label test pressing				
☐	Bucketfull Of Brains	(no number)		UK	2/92

Warner Brothers 1378

Warner Brothers PRO 607

REM Fan Club single 1990

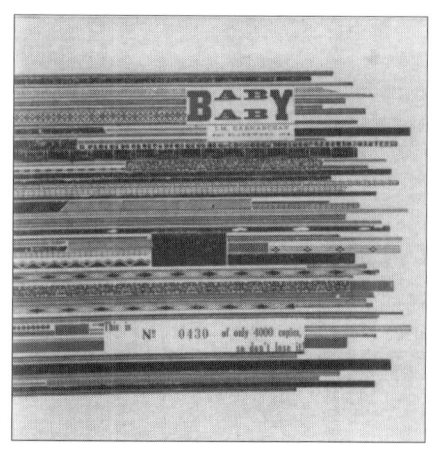

REM Fan Club single 1991

COMMERCIALLY ISSUED 12"
SINGLES AND EPS

Talk About The Passion/Shaking Through/Carnival Of Sorts (Box Cars)/
1,000,000
☐ IRS   PFSX 1026   ■   UK   11/83
So. Central Rain (I'm Sorry)/Voice Of Harold/Pale Blue Eyes
☐ IRS   IRSX 105   ■   UK   3/84
☐ IRS   A12.4255   ■   NL   3/84
(Don't Go Back To) Rockville/Wolves/9-9 (live)/Gardening At Night (live)
☐ IRS   IRSX 107   ■   UK   6/84
☐ IRS   ILSA12.4734   ■   NL   6/84
☐ Illegal   A12.4734   ■   SPAIN   /84
         NOTE: Spanish issue above has different colour tint on sleeve Live cuts on all three above
         recorded in mono, at L'Eldorado, Paris, France 20/4/84.
Can't Get There From Here (extended mix)/Bandwagon/Burning Hell
☐ IRS   IRT 102   ■   UK   7/85
         NOTE: cover says "extended mix" but version is same as LP.
Can't Get There From Here (extended mix)/Bandwagon/Burning Hell
☐ IRS   ILSA12-6384   ■   NL   /85
         NOTE: Some copies with tour date sticker. Others say "Special edit - plus 2 new songs".
         The 'Special edit' is, nevertheless, identical to the album version.
Wendell Gee/Crazy/Driver 8 (live)
☐ IRS   IRT 105   ■   UK   10/85
Wendell Gee/Driver 8 (live)/Ages Of You/Burning Down
☐ IRS   ILSA12.6587   ■   NL   9/85
Fall On Me/Rotary Ten/Toys In The Attic
☐ IRS   IRMT 121   ■   UK   7/86
Superman/White Tornado/Femme Fatale
☐ IRS   IRMT 128   ■   UK   /86
Superman/White Tornado/Perfect Circle
☐ IRS   ILS 650255 6   ■   NL   4/86
It's The End Of The World As We Know It (And I Feel Fine)/This One Goes
Out (live)/Maps And Legends (live)
☐ IRS   IRMT 145   ■   UK   8/87
         NOTE: Live cuts recorded at McCabe's Guitar Shop, San Francisco 24/5/87
The One I Love/Last Date (live)/Disturbance At The Heron House
☐ IRS   IRMT 146   ■   UK   11/87
☐ IRS   ILS 6511136   ■   NL   /87
The One I Love/The One I Love (live)/Maps And Legends (live)
☐ IRS   IRS 23792   ■   USA   8/87
Finest Worksong (lengthy club mix)/Finest Worksong (other mix)/Time After
Time etc (live)
☐ IRS   IRS 23850   ■   USA   3/88
☐ IRS   IRMT 161   ■   UK   4/88
☐ IRS   ILS 651320 6   ■   NL   4/88
The One I Love/Fall On Me/So. Central Rain (I'm Sorry)
☐ IRS   IRMT 173   ■   UK   10/88

	Stand/Memphis Train Blues/The Eleventh Untitled Song (Instrumental version)				
☐	Warner Brothers	W7577T	■	UK	1/89
	Orange Crush/Ghost Riders /Dark Globe				
☐	Warner Brothers	W2960T	■	UK	5/89
	Stand/Pop Song 89 (acoustic version)/Skintight (live)				
	NOTE: Live track recorded at Orlando Arena, Florida, USA, 30/4/89				
☐	Warner Brothers	W2833T	■	UK	8/89
	Losing My Religion/Rotary 11/After Hours (live)				
	NOTE: Live track recorded at the Fox Theatre, Atlanta, GA, USA, 13/11/89, from the 'Tourfilm' soundtrack				
☐	Warner Bros	W0015T	■	UK	/91
	Shiny Happy People/Forty Second Song/Losing My Religion (live acoustic version)				
☐	Warner Bros	W0027T	■	UK	/91
	Near Wild Heaven/Pop Song 89 (live)/Half A World Away (live acoustic version)				
	NOTE: Live tracks recorded (i) at the Borderline, London, UK 15/3/91 (ii) for 'Rockline', Los Angeles, CA, USA 1/4/91.				
☐	Warner Bros	W0055T	■	UK	8/91
	Radio Song/Love Is All Around (live)/Shiny Happy People (Music mix)				
	NOTE: Live track recorded for 'Rockline', Los Angeles, CA, USA, 1/4/91				
☐	Warner Brothers	W0072T	■	UK	11/91
	Radio Song (Tower Of Luv Bug Mix)/Love Is All Around (live)/Belong (live)				
	NOTE: Live tracks recorded at (i) 'Rockline', Los Angeles, CA, USA, 1/4/91. (ii) Coliseum, Greensboro, NC, USA 10/11/89 for 'This Film Is On' soundtrack.				
☐	Warner Brothers	9 40229-0	■	USA	11/91
☐	Warner Brothers	9362-40229-0	■	GE	11/91
	Losing My Religion/Fretless/Losing My Religion (live acoustic version)/Rotary Eleven				
	NOTE: 'Song Of The Year' on cover. Live track recorded for 'Rockline', Los Angeles, CA, USA, 1/4/91				
☐	Warner Brothers	9362-40399-0	■	GE	/92
	Drive/World Leader Pretend/First We Take Manhattan				
☐	Warner Brothers	9362-40634-0	■	GE	9/92

IRS PFSX 1026

IRS IRMT 121

IRS IRMT 145

IRS IRMT 146

IRS IRMT 161

Warner Brothers W2833T

PROMOTIONAL AND OTHER NON-COMMERCIAL 12" SINGLES & EPS

☐ Talk About The Passion/Catapult/Sitting Still
IRS   SP 70966   USA   /83

☐ Pretty Persuasion/(Don't Go Back To) Rockville (edited, 3.54)
IRS   SP 70979   USA   /84

☐ (Don't Go Back To) Rockville (special radio edit,3.54)/Catapult (live)
IRS   SP 70982   ■   USA   /84
  NOTE: Live B-side recorded at Seattle, WA, USA 27/6/84

☐ Can't Get There From Here (radio edit, 3.09)/Driver 8/Life And How To Live It
IRS   L33-17004   ■   USA   /85

☐ Driver 8/Driver 8 (live)
IRS   L33-17034   ■   USA   /85
  NOTE: Live recording from Seattle, WA, USA 27/6/84

☐ Fall On Me/same
IRS   L33-17159   ■   USA   /85

☐ Life And How To Live It/Bandwagon/Crazy
IRS   L33-17060   ■   USA   /85

☐ Fall On Me/Rotary Ten/Toys In The Attic
IRS   IRMT 121 dl   UK   9/86

☐ I Believe/Toys In The Attic
IRS   L33-17199   ■   USA   /86

☐ Superman/same
IRS   L33-17200   ■   USA   11/86

☐ Ages Of You/same
IRS   SP 70416   ■   USA   /87

☐ The One I Love/same
☐ IRS   L33-17384   ■   USA   /87
☐ IRS   WIRMT 173ADL   UK   /87

☐ It's The End Of The World As We Know It (And I Feel Fine)/Disturbance At The Heron House(live)
IRS   L33-17430   ■   USA   /87

☐ Finest Worksong (media version)/Finest Worksong (untouched version)
IRS   L33-17510   ■   USA   /88

☐ Finest Worksong (other mix)/Time After Time Etc/Finest Worksong (lengthy club mix)
IRS   WIRM(T) 161B DL   ■   UK   /88

☐ Orange Crush/same
Warner Brothers   PRO-A-3306   ■   USA   /88
  NOTE: Pressed in translucent orange vinyl with picture label

☐ Deck The Halls
Warner Brothers   PRO-A-3328   ■   USA   /89
  NOTE: Green vinyl pressing.

☐ Stand/(other artists)
Warner Brothers   PROMO 352   ITALY   /89
  NOTE: label says 'promomix' (sic)

PAGE 26

IRS SP 70982

IRS L33-17004

IRS L33-17034

IRS L33-17060

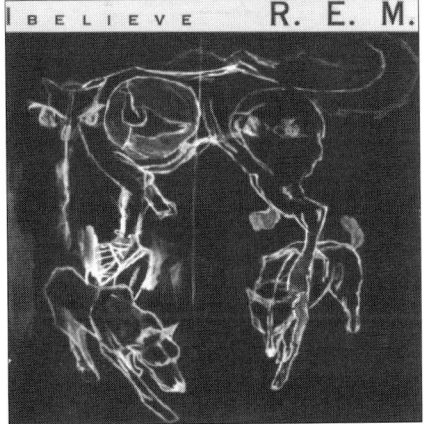
IRS L33-17199

IRS L33-17510

	Shiny Happy People (Music mix)/Shiny Happy People (Hip mix)/ Shiny Happy People (Pop mix)			
☐	Warner Brothers	PRO-A-5060	USA	/91
	Shiny Happy People (Dance To The Music mix)/Shiny Happy People (Hip mix)/Shiny Happy People (Pop mix)			
☐	Warner Brothers	PRO-A-5660	USA	/91
	Radio Song (Tower Of Luv Bug mix)/Radio Song (Monster mix)			
☐	Warner Brothers	PRO-A-5263 ■	USA	/91

IRS WIRM(T) 161B DL   Warner Brothers PRO-A-5263

COMMERCIALLY AVAILABLE ALBUMS AND MINI-ALBUMS

☐	"Chronic Town" (mini-LP)	IRS	SP 70502	USA	8/82
	SIDE 1: Wolves Lower, Gardening At Night, Carnival Of Sorts (Boxcars).				
	SIDE 2: 1,000,000, Stumble.				
	NOTE: Original US pressing has picture label showing gargoyle's head as per album sleeve.				
☐	"Chronic Town" (mini-LP)	IRS	ILP 26097	NL	1984
☐	"Chronic Town" (mini-LP)	IRS	SP 70502	CAN	1984
☐	"Murmur"	IRS	SP 70014	USA	4/83
	SIDE 1: Radio Free Europe, Pilgrimage, Laughing, Talk About The Passion, Moral Kiosk, Perfect Circle.				
	SIDE 2: Catapult, Sitting Still, 9-9, Shaking Through, We Walk, West Of The Fields				
☐	"Murmur"	IRS	SP 70604	USA	1983
☐	"Murmur"	IRS	SP 70604	CAN	1983
☐	"Murmur"	IRS	SP 70604	UK	8/83
☐	"Murmur"	Illegal	ILP 25433	NL	1983
☐	"Murmur"	CBS/Sony	25 AP-2659	JAP	1983
☐	"Murmur"	IRS/CBS	ILP 465378 1	NL	1991
	(CBS 'Nice Price' re-issue)				
☐	"Reckoning"	IRS	SP 70044	USA	4/84
	SIDE 1: Harborcoat, Seven Chinese Brothers, So. Central Rain (I'm Sorry), Pretty				

Persuasion, Time After Time (Annelise).
SIDE 2: Second Guessing, Letter Never Sent, Camera, (Don't Go Back To) Rockville, Little America.
Note: some copies in green vinyl, others in violet.

☐ "Reckoning"	IRS	IRSA 7045	UK	4/84
☐ "Reckoning"	IRS	SP 70044	CAN	1984
☐ "Reckoning"	Illegal	☐ILP 25915	SPAIN	1984
☐ "Reckoning"	IRS	28 AP 2847 (IR)	JAP	1984
☐ "Reckoning"	IRS	ILP 25915	NL	1984
☐ "Reckoning"	Illegal	ELPS 4439	NZ	1984
☐ **"Reckoning"**	**IRS**	**CBS 25915**	**ISRAEL**	**198?**
☐ "Reckoning"	IRS/CBS	ILP 465379 1	NL	1991

(CBS 'Nice Price' re-issue)

☐ **"Fables Of The Reconstruction"**   IRS   IRS 5592   USA   6/85
SIDE 1: Feeling Gravity's Pull, Maps And Legends, Driver 8, Life And How To Live It, Old Man Kensey.
SIDE 2: Can't Get There From Here, Green Grow The Rushes, Kohoutek, Auctioneer (Another Engine), Good Advices, Wendell Gee.

☐ **"Fables Of The Reconstruction"**	IRS	MIRF 1003	UK☐	6/85
☐ **"Fables Of The Reconstruction"**	IRS	IRS 5592	CAN	1985
☐ **"Fables Of The Reconstruction"**	IRS	ILP 26525	NL	1985
☐ **"Fables Of The Reconstruction"**	IRS	IRS 26525	SPAIN	1985
☐ **"Fables Of The Reconstruction"**	IRS	IRS 26525	PORT	1985
☐ **"Fables Of The Reconstruction"**	IRS	IRS 28 AP 3058 (IR)JAP		1985
☐ **"Fables Of The Reconstruction"**	Epic	144.877	BRAZIL	1985
☐ **"Fables Of The Reconstruction"**	Epic	QEL 25105	PHIL	198?
☐ **"Fables Of The Reconstruction"**	IRS	IRS 26525	ISRAEL	198?

NOTE: Regular sleeve but with small Hebrew script on reverse.

☐ **"Fables Of The Reconstruction"**
(CBS 'Nice Price' re-issue)   IRS/CBS   ILP 465380 1   NL   1991

☐ **"Life's Rich Pageant"**   IRS   IRS 5783   USA   7/86
SIDE 1: Begin The Begin, These Days, Fall On Me, Cuyahoga, Hyena, Underneath The Bunker.
SIDE 2: The Flowers Of Guatemala, I Believe, What If We Give It Away?, Just A Touch, Swan Swan H., Superman.

☐ **"Life's Rich Pageant"**	IRS	MIRG 1014	UK	8/86
☐ **"Life's Rich Pageant"**	IRS	IRS 5783	CAN	1986
☐ **"Life's Rich Pageant"**	IRS	ILP 57064	NL	1986
☐ **"Life's Rich Pageant"**	Epic	144.905	BRAZIL	1986
☐ **"Life's Rich Pageant"**	IRS/CBS	ILP 45381 1	NL	1991

(CBS 'Nice price' re-issue)

☐ "Dead Letter Office"(compilation)IRS   SP 70054   USA   4/87
SIDE 1: Crazy, There She Goes Again, Burning Down, Voice Of Harold, Burning Hell, White Tornado, Toys In The Attic.
SIDE 2: Windout, Ages Of You, Pale Blue Eyes, Rotary Ten, Bandwagon, Femme Fatale, Walter's Theme, King Of The Road.

☐ "Dead Letter Office"	IRS	SP 70054	UK	5/87
☐ "Dead Letter Office"	IRS	SP 70054	CAN	1987
☐ "Dead Letter Office"	Epic	235.502	BRAZIL	1987
☐ "Dead Letter Office"	IRS	ILP 450961	GE	1987
☐ "Dead Letter Office"	IRS/CBS	ILP 465382 1	NL	1991

(CBS 'Nice Price' re-issue)

☐	"Document"	IRS	IRS 42059	USA	9/87

SIDE 1: Finest Worksong, Welcome To The Occupation, Exhuming McCarthy, Disturbance At The Heron House, Strange, It's The End Of The World As We Know It (And I Feel Fine)
SIDE 2: The One I Love, Fireplace, Lightnin' Hopkins, King Of Birds, Oddfellows Local 151.

☐	"Document"	IRS	MIRG 1025	UK	10/87
☐	"Document"	IRS	IRS 42059	CAN	1987
☐	"Document"	IRS	28 AP 3382	JAPAN	1987
☐	"Document"	IRS	ILP 460105	NL	1987
☐	"Document"	IRS	ILP 460105	AUST	1987
☐	"Document"	IRS/CBS	ILP 465383 1	NL	1991

(CBS 'Nice Price' re-issue)

☐	"Eponymous" (compilation)	IRS	IR 6262	USA	10/88

SIDE 1: Radio Free Europe (original Hib Tone version), Gardening At Night (different vocal mix), Talk About The Passion, So. Central Rain (I'm Sorry), (Don't Go Back To) Rockville, Can't Get There From Here.
SIDE 2: Driver 8, Romance, Fall On Me, The One I Love, Finest Worksong (mutual drum horn mix), It's The End Of The World As We Know It (And I Feel Fine).

☐	"Eponymous"	IRS	MIRG 1038	UK	10/88
☐	"Eponymous"	IRS	463 147 1	GE	1988
☐	"Eponymous"	IRS	ILP 463147 1	NL	1988
☐	"Eponymous"	IRS/CBS	ILP 465384 1	UK	1991

(CBS 'Nice Price' re-issue)

☐	"Green"	Warner Brothers	25795-1	USA	11/88

SIDE 1: Pop Song 89, Get Up, You Are The Everything, Stand, World Leader Pretend, The Wrong Child.
SIDE 2: Orange Crush, Turn You Inside Out, Hair Shirt, I Remember California, (Untitled).

☐	"Green"	Warner Brothers	WX-234	UK	11/88
☐	"Green"	Warner Brothers	670.8035	BRAZIL	11/88
☐	"Green"	Warner Brothers	925 795	GE	11/88
☐	"Green"	Warner Brothers	925 795	SPAIN	11/88
☐	"Green"	Warner Brothers	BAN 925 795	ISRAEL	11/88

☐	"Out Of Time"	Warner Brothers	26496-1	USA	3/91

SIDE 1: Radio Song, Losing My Religion, Low, Near Wild Heaven, Endgame.
SIDE 2: Shiny happy People, Belong, Half A World Away, Texarkana, Country Feedback, Me In Honey.

☐	"Out Of Time"	Warner Brothers	WX 404	UK	3/91
☐	"Out Of Time"	Warner Brothers	7599-26496-1	GE	3/91

NOTE: Initial copies included free 7" PRO-610 featuring: World Leader Pretend (live)/ Turn You Inside Out (live) both from 'Tourfilm' soundtrack.

☐	"The Best Of REM" (compilation)	IRS	MIRH 1 AL	UK	9/91

SIDE 1: Carnival Of Sorts, Radio Free Europe, Perfect Circle, Talk About The Passion, So. Central Rain, Pretty Persuasion, Green Grow The Rushes.
SIDE 2: Can't Get There From Here, Fall On Me, I Believe, Cuyahoga, The One I Love, Finest Worksong, It's The End Of The World As We Know It (And I Feel Fine).

☐	"The Best Of REM' (compilaton)	Hispavox	082-713-1281	SPAIN	10/91
☐	"The Best Of REM" (compilation)	IRS	7.131281	GE	/91

Chronic Town

Murmur

Reckoning

Fables Of The Reconstruction

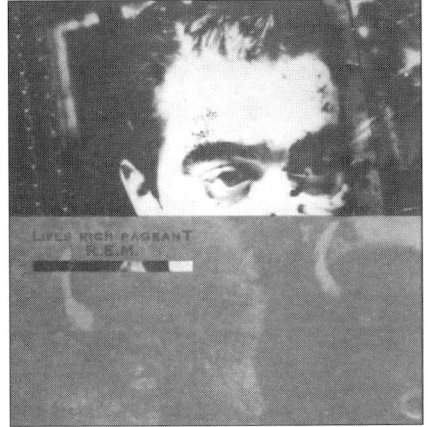
Life's Rich Pageant

Dead Letter Office

Document

Eponymous

Green

Out Of Time

The Best Of R.E.M.

Automatic For The People

☐ "The Best of R.E.M." (compilation) EMI/Sony 11001437 COLUMBIA /91

☐ "Automatic For The People" Warner Brothers 9362-45055-1 UK 10/92
SIDE 1: Drive, Try Not To Breathe, The Sidewinder Sleeps Tonight, Everybody Hurts, New Orleans Instrumental No.1, Sweetness Follows.
SIDE 2: Monty Got A Raw Deal, Ignoreland, Star Me Kitten, Man On The Moon, Nightswimming, Find The River.

INTERVIEW LPS

These discs feature the spoken word only, there is no musical content whatsoever.

☐ untitled (Picture Disc) Baktabak BAK 2057 UK 10/87
SIDE 1: Picadilly radio interview with 'Tony The Greek' 17/11/84.
SIDE 2: Picadilly radio interview with 'Tony The Greek' 23/6/85

☐ "Rapid Mouth Movement" Pow Wow POW 01 UK /88
SIDE 1: Interview with Michael Stipe
SIDE 2: Interview with Michael Stipe

☐ "Audio.Visual" Bespoke BSPLP 001 UK 12/91
SIDE 1: Interview with Michael Stipe & Peter Buck, 11/83.
SIDE 2; Interview with Michael Stipe & Peter Buck, 11/83.
(Limited edition of 1,500 with 24 page booklet)

INTERVIEW CDS

These discs feature the spoken word only, there is no musical content whatsoever.

☐ "Shiny Chatty People" Baktabak CBAK 4041 UK 5/91
(interviews with 'Tony The Greek' on Piccadilly Radio 17/11/84 & 23/6/85)

☐ "Audio.Visual" Bespoke BSP 001 UK 11/91
(interview with Stipe & Buck by John Platt from November 1983 within full colour fold-out digi-pak incorporating a 72 page book)

PROMOTIONAL & OTHER NON-COMMERCIAL ALBUMS

☐ "Should We Talk About The Weather"
Warner Brothers PRO-A-3377 USA /88
(Promo only double LP. Interviews with REM and featuring cuts from "Green": Pop Song 89, Stand, Orange Crush, Get Up, You Are The Everything, The Wrong Child, Hairshirt, World Leader Pretend, Turn You Inside Out, I Remember California, Untitled)

RADIO PROMOTIONAL ALBUMS
(All are single albums unless noted otherwise)

☐ **"Live Radio Concert"** (double LP)
The Source Concert, NBC   84-28   USA   /84
(Recorded live at Seattle Music Hall, Washington, USA 27/6/84. Features: Moral Kiosk, Driver 8, Catapult, Hyena, Camera, Pilgrimage, Talk About The Passion, Seven Chinese Brothers, So. Central Rain (I'm Sorry), Pretty Pursuasion, Gardening At Night, 9-9, Wind Out, Old Man Kensey, Radio Free Europe, Little America, Sitting Still, Burning Down, Pale Blue Eyes, 1,000,000, So You Want To Be A Rock'n'Roll Star, Carnival Of Sorts (Box Cars), Marble Table).

☐ **"PFM Guest DJ Series"**
GDJ 84-133   Show # 133   USA   10/84
(Peter Buck is the guest DJ on this disc which includes previously released cuts by: REM ("So. Central Rain (I'm Sorry)", "Little America", "Windout" and "Radio Free Europe"), Jason & The Scorchers, Shangri Las, The Fleshtones, Sly & The Family Stone, Let's Active, Chuck Berry, The Cramps and The Rain Parade.

☐ **"BBC Rock Hour"**
London Wavelength   BC 603☐   USA   1/85
(Recorded live at Rock City, Nottingham, UK 21/11/84. Features: Hyena, Talk About The Passion, (Don't Go Back To) Rockville, Auctioneer, So. Central rain (I'm Sorry), Sitting Still, Old Man Kensey, Gardening At Night, 9-9, Wind Out, Driver 8, Pretty Persuasion, Radio Free Europe).

☐ **"In Concert"**
BBC Transcription Services   CN 4516/S   UK   5/85
(Recorded as per "BBC Rock Hour" above. Features all above tracks plus: West Of The Fields)

☐ **"REM '85"**
Innerview Series #33   Show # 13   USA   /85
(Michael Stipe interview hosted by Jim Ladd)

☐ **"In Concert"** (double LP)
Westwood One Radio Networks   IC-86--24 USA   USA   11/86
(Features REM & The Alarm, recorded live at Rock City, Nottingham, UK 21/11/84). REM: West of the Fields, (Don't Go Back To) Rockville, Auctioneer, So. Central Rain (I'm Sorry), Sitting Still, Driver 8, 9-9, Wind Out, Pretty Persuasion, Radio Free Europe.

☐ **"Off The Record Special"** (double LP)
Westwood One Radio Networks   Show #89-09   USA   2/89
(Mary Turner interviews REM. Following album cuts featured: These Days, Get Up, Stand, Catapult, Hyena, Orange Crush, I Believe, So. Central Rain (I'm Sorry), Superman, Fall On Me, The One I Love, Turn You Inside Out, Finest Worksong, It's The End Of The World As We Know It (And I Feel Fine), Pop Song 89).

☐ **"Timothy White's Rock Stars"** (double LP)
Westwood One Radio Networks   WO 89-C   USA   3/89
(Interviews with REM. Following album cuts featured: Stand, World Leader Pretend, Get Up, Radio Free Europe, (Don't Go Back To) Rockville, Perfect Circle, The One I Love, Fall On Me, Can't Get There From Here, It's The End Of The World As We Know It (And I Feel Fine), Pop Song 89 (unreleased demo version), Orange Crush).

☐ **"The 1989 Isle Of Dreams Festival"**
Westwood One Radio Networks				USA			9/89
(US series of albums for radio promo only, covering the Isle Of Dreams festival, 1989. Side 6 features REM: Finest Worksong, Pop Song 89, Stand).

☐ **"In Concert"** (Triple LP)
Westwood One Radio Networks		IC-89-		USA			/89
(Recorded live in Orlando, Florida, USA 30th April 1989. Features: Pop Song 89, Exhuming McCarthy, Welcome To The Occupation, Disturbance At The Heron House, Turn You Inside Out, Orange Crush, Feeling Gravity's Pull, Begin The Begin, Pretty Persuasion, I Believe, Swan Swan H, Skin Tight, King Of Birds, Crazy, Finest Worksong, You Are The Everything, Academy Fight Song, Stand, Perfect Circle, Get Up, It's The End Of The World As We Know It (And I Feel Fine)).
NB: This set also available as a double album, with less jingles/adverts etc.

☐ **"Stars Of The Superstars"** (triple LP)
Westwood One Radio Networks		CO-89-33	USA			/89
(Side 5 features REM with live versions of: Pop Song '89, Orange Crush & It's The End Of The World As We Know It (And I Feel Fine). Other featured artists include The Who, Rod Stewart and Jackson Browne. It could have been worse...)

☐ **"Off The Record Special"** (double LP)
Westwood One Radio Networks		Show #91-20	USA			5/91
(Mary Turner interviews Peter Buck. Following album cuts featured: Get Up, Orange Crush, Me In Honey, Low, It's The End Of The World As We Know It (And I Feel Fine), Stand, Fall On Me, Radio Song, Pop Song '89, (Don't Go Back To) Rockville, Belong, Shiny Happy People, The One I Love, Finest Worksong, Losing My Religion).

RADIO PROMOTIONAL CDS

☐ **"Up Close"**
Media American Radio			89-08		USA			3/89
(Interviews with REM. Following album cuts featured: Turn You Inside Out, Pop Song 89, Stand, Radio Free Europe, (Don't Go Back To) Rockville, Perfect Circle, The One I Love, Fall On Me, Can't Get There From Here, Fall On Me, Superman, It's The End Of The World As We Know It (And I Feel Fine), The One I Love, Oddfellows Local 151, Finest Worksong, Exhuming McCarthy, Ages Of You, World Leader Pretend, Orange Crush).

☐ **"Up Close"**
Media America, iNC			91-13		USA			/91
(A double CD set. The following album cuts are featured: DISC 1: Radio Song, Losing My Religion, Near Wild Heaven, Radio Free Europe, So. Central Rain (I'm Sorry), (Don't Go Back To) Rockville, Driver 8, Can't Get There From Here, Fall On Me (unreleased live version), Superman, It's The End Of The World As We Know It (And I Fewel Fine). DISC 2: The One I Love, Oddfellows Local 151, Finest Worksong, Ages Of You, Stand, Turn You Inside Out, Pop Song 89, World Leader Pretend, Orange Crush, Shiny Happy People, Texarkana)

COMMERCIALLY ISSUED COMPACT DISC SINGLES AND EPS

(All CDs are 5" unless noted otherwise)

☐ **The One I Love/Last date/Disturbance At The Heron House (live)**
　IRS　　　　　　　　　　DIRM 146　　　　UK　　　　　　11/87
　　　NOTE: The tracks are incorrectly listed on the disc as: End Of The World/Finest Worksong/The One I Love.

The One I Love/The One I Love (live)/Maps & Legends (live)
　　　NOTE: Live tracks recorded at McCabe's Guitar Shop, Santa Monica, CA, USA 24/5/87
☐　IRS　　　　　　　　　　1C (560) 2045372　　GE　　　　　　/88

Finest Worksong (other mix)/same (lengthy club mix)/Time After Time Etc
　　　NOTE: 3" CD
☐　IRS　　　　　　　　　　ILS 651320 2　　　　NL　　　　　　4/88

Finest Worksong (LP version)/Time After Time Etc/It's The End Of The World As We Know It (And I Feel Fine)
☐　IRS　　　　　　　　　　DIRM 161　　　　UK　　　　　　4/88
　　　NOTE: Limited edition boxed set

The One I Love/So. Central Rain (I'm Sorry)/Fall On Me
☐　IRS　　　　　　　　　　DIRM 173　　　　UK　　　　　　　/88

Stand/Memphis Train Blues (Eleventh Untitled Song)
☐　Warner Brothers　　　　W7577CD　　　　UK　　　　　　1/89
　　　NOTE: 3" CD in standard packaging
☐　Warner Brothers　　　　W7577CDX　　　UK　　　　　　1/89
　　　NOTE: 3" CD single/limited edition maple-leaf pack.

Stand/Memphis Train Blues
☐　Warner Brothers　　　　10P3-6078　　　　JAPAN　　　　　/89
　　　NOTE: 3" CD in card pack

Stand/Memphis Train Blues
☐　Warner Brothers　　　　7599-27688-2　　USA　　　　　　　/89
　　　NOTE: 3" CD in card pack

Orange Crush/Ghost Riders/Dark Globe
☐　Warner Brothers　　　　W2960CD　　　　UK　　　　　　5/89
　　　NOTE: 3" CD

Stand/Pop Song 89 (acoustic)/Skin Tight (live)
☐　Warner Brothers　　　　W2833CD　　　　UK　　　　　　8/89
　　　NOTE: 3" CD

Stand/Pop Song 89 (acoustic)/Skin Tight (live)
☐　Warner Brothers　　　　W2833CDX　　　UK　　　　　　8/89
　　　NOTE: 3" CD/Special limited edition wrap-over sleeve.

Losing My Religion/Rotary Eleven/After Hours (live)
　　　NOTE: Live track recorded at Fox Theatre, Atlanta, GA, USA 13/11/89, from the 'Tourfilm' soundtrack.
☐　Warner Brothers　　　　W0015CD　　　　UK　　　　　　2/91

Losing My Religion/Stand (live)/Turn You Inside Out (live)/World Leader Pretend (live)
　　　NOTE: Live tracks recorded 11/89, from 'Tourfilm' soundtrack.
☐　Warner Brothers　　　　W0015CDX　　　UK　　　　　　2/91

Shiny Happy People/Forty Second Song/Losing My Religion (live acoustic version)
　　　NOTE: Live track recorded for 'Rockline' in Los Angeles, CA, USA, 1/4/91
☐　Warner Brothers　　　　W0027CD　　　　UK　　　　　　5/91

PAGE 36

**Shiny Happy People/I Remember California (live)/Get Up (live)/
Pop Song '89 (live)**
    NOTE: Live tracks recorded 11/89 from the 'Tourfilm' soundtrack
☐   Warner Bros   W0027CDX   UK   5/91

Near Wild Heaven/Tom's Diner (live)/Low (live)/Endgame (live)
☐   Warner Bros   W0055CDX   UK   8/91
    NOTE: Live tracks recorded at the Borderline, London, UK, 15/3/91

**"It's The End Of The World As We Know It (And I Feel Fine)" Volume Two
It's The End Of The World as We Know It (And I Feel Fine)/Radio Free Europe
(Hib-Tone version)/Last Date (live)(recorded 4/9/87 at John Keane Studios)/
White Tornado.**
☐   IRS   DIRMX 180   UK   /91
    NOTE: The above issue may be withdrawn, but copies have still come onto the market

The One I Love/This One Goes Out (live)/Maps And Legends (live)
☐   IRS   DIRMT 178   UK   9/91
    NOTE: Package includes a 'biography'. Don't hold your breath.

The One I Love/Driver 8 (live)/Disturbance At The Heron House (live)/Crazy
    NOTE: Live tracks recorded at McCabe's Guitar Shop, Santa Monica, CA, USA, 24/5/87
    Package includes 'discography' (laughabie really!)
☐   IRS   DIRMX 178   UK   9/91

**Radio Song/You Are The Everything (live)/Orange Crush (live)/
Belong (live)**
    NOTE: Live tracks from (i) 11/89, 'Tourfilm'soundtrack (ii) 11/89 (iii) Coliseum, Greensboro, NC,
    USA 10/11/89 from 'This Film Is On'soundtrack.
    Includes free slip-case to contain other 'live' CDs in same series.
☐   Warner Brothers   W0072CDX   UK   11/91
☐   Warner Brothers   4362-40229-2   GE   11/91

**Radio Song (Tower Of Love Bug Mix)/Love Is All Around (live)/
Belong (live)**
    NOTE: Live tracks from (i) 'Rockline', Los Angeles, CA, USA 1/4/91.(ii) Coliseum,
    Greensboro, NC, USA 10/11/89 from 'This Film Is On' soundtrack.
☐   Warner Brothers   9 40229-2   USA   11/91

"REM Singles Collection"
    NOTE: 4 CD set in slip case, including the following CDs above:
    W0015CDX, W0027CDX, W0055CDX, W0072CDX
☐   Warner Brothers   9362-40313-2   GE   /91
☐   Warner Brothers   WPCP-4781   JAPAN   /91
    NOTE: same as above but all Cds are Japanese. Comes complete with stickers.

**Losing My Religion/Fretless/Losing My Religion (live acoustic version)/Rotary
Eleven**
    NOTE: 'Song of the Year' on cover. Live track recorded for 'Rockline', Los Angeles,
    CA, USA, 1/4/91.
☐   Warner Brothers   9362-40399-2   GE   2/92

Drive/Winged Mammal Theme
☐   Warner Brothers   2-18729   USA   9/92
    NOTE: Available with four different front covers to insert - each featuring a picture of a
    different member of the band.

Drive/World Leader Pretend/First We Take Manhattan
☐   Warner Brothers   9362-40634-2   GE   9/92

**Drive/First We Take Manhattan/Winged Mammal Theme/It's A Free World
Baby**
    NOTE: Marked "Collectors edition CD"
☐   Warner Brothers   9362-40633-2   GE   9/92

PROMOTIONAL & OTHER NON-COMMERCIAL COMPACT DISC SINGLES

(All CDs are 5″)

It's The End Of The World As We Know It (And I Feel Fine)/Finest Worksong/ The One I Love
☐ IRS   DIRM 146   UK   /87

It's The End Of The World As We Know It (And I Feel Fine)(edited version)/ same (LP version)
☐ IRS   CD45-17476   USA   /87

Orange Crush (picture disc)
☐ Warner Brothers   PRO-CD 3306   USA   /88

Stand
☐ Warner Brothers   PRO-CD 3353   USA   1/89

Pop Song 89
☐ Warner Brothers   PRO-CD 3357   USA   5/89

Turn You Inside Out
☐ Warner Brothers   PRO-CD 3446   USA   /89

Get Up (LP version)/Orange Crush (live)/Turn You Inside Out (live)
☐ Warner Brothers   PRO-CD 3716   USA   /90
NOTE: Live tracks recorded in Orlando, Florida 30/4/89

Get Up (live)/World Leader Pretend (live)/It's The End Of The World As We Know It (And I Feel Fine)(live)
NOTE: 'Get Up' video from 'Tourfilm'. Live tracks recorded 11/89 from 'Tourfilm' soundtrack.
☐ Warner Brothers   PRO-CDV-4460   USA   /90

Losing My Religion (wood-grain effect picture disc)
☐ Warner Brothers   PRO-CD-4707   USA   /91

Radio Song
☐ Warner Brothers   PRO-CD-4808   USA   /91

Texarcana (striped effect picture disc)
☐ Warner Brothers   PRO-CD-4826   USA   /91

Losing My Religion (live acoustic version)
NOTE: Live track from 'Rockline' Los Angeles, CA, USA 1/4/91
☐ Warner Brothers   PRO-CD-4881   USA   /91

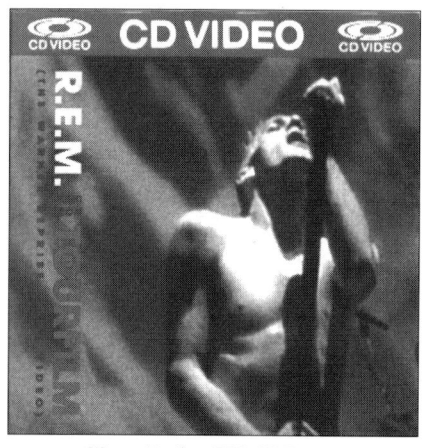

Warner Brothers PRO-CDV-4460    *Warner Brothers PRO-2002-2*

☐	**Shiny Happy People (wood-grain effect picture disc)**			
	Warner Brothers	PRO-CD-	USA	/91
☐	**Near Wild Heaven**			
	Warner Brothers	PRO-CD-5058	USA	/91

**Shiny Happy People (Music mix)/Shiny Happy People (Pop mix)/
Shiny Happy People (Hip mix)**
☐ Warner Brothers   PRO-CD-5060   USA   /91

**Half A World Away (live acoustic version)/Love Is All Around
(live acoustic version)/Losing My Religion (live acoustic version)**
   NOTE: Only issued to subscribers to the French Rock magazine "Les Inrockuptibles"
   Live tracks all taken from 'Rockline' Los Angeles, CA, USA, 1/4/91.
☐ Warner Brothers   PRO-2002-2   FR   /91

**Finest Worksong/The One I Love/It's The End Of The World As We Know It
(And I Feel Fine)/Finest Worksong (lengthy club mix)**
☐ IRS   REM1   UK   /92
   NOTE: Individually numbered promo. Cover says: "Sampler from 'The Best Of R.E.M."

PROMOTIONAL & OTHER NON-COMMERCIAL COMPACT DISC ALBUMS

☐ **"An AOR Radio Staple" (promo only compilation)**
   IRS   IRSD-SEVEN   USA   /87
   (It's The End Of The World As We Know It (And I Feel Fine), The One I Love,
   Fall On Me, I Believe, Pretty Persuasion, So. Central
   Rain (I'm Sorry), Superman, Driver 8, Can't Get There From Here,
   Talk About The Passion, Radio Free Europe)

☐ **"Should We Talk About The Weather"**
   Warner Brothers   PRO-CD 3377   USA   /89
   (Promo only CD. Interviews with REM and featuring cuts from "Green":
   Pop Song 89, Stand, Orange Crush, Get Up, You Are The Everything,
   The Wrong Child, Hairshirt, World Leader Pretend, Turn You Inside Out,
   I Remember California, Untitled)

☐ **"Green"**
   Warner Brothers   PRO-CD 3292   USA   /88
   (In green cloth cover with unique fold-out insert. Same tracks as normal CD release)

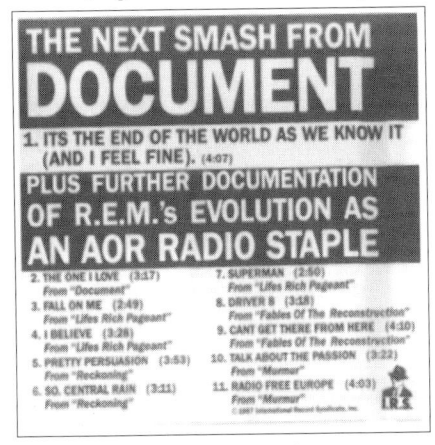

An AOR Radio Staple   *Should We Talk About The Weather*

COMMERCIALLY ISSUED COMPACT DISC ALBUMS

(All track lists as per equivalent vinyl discs)

☐ "Murmur"	IRS	AM 70014	USA	/83
☐ "Murmur"	IRS	CD 70014	UK	/89
☐ "Murmur"	IRS	CSCS-6080	JAP	/8?
☐ "Murmur"	IRS	CDMID 129	UK	3/91

(A&M mid-price re-issue)

☐ "Murmur"	IRS/CBS	465378 2	NL	/91

(CBS mid-price reissue)

☐ "Murmur"	IRS	0777 7 13158 2 4	GE	8/92

+ extra tracks: There She Goes Again, 9-9 (live), Gardening at Night (live), Catapult (live)

☐ "Reckoning"	IRS	AM 70044	USA	/84
☐ "Reckoning"	IRS	CD 70044	UK	/89
☐ "Reckoning"	IRS	CDA 7045	UK	/89
☐ "Reckoning"	IRS	CSCS-6081	JAP	/8?
☐ "Reckoning"	IRS/CBS	465379 2	NL	/91

(CBS mid-price re-issue)

☐ "Reckoning"	IRS	7-13159-2	GE	8/92

+ extra tracks: Wind Out (with friends)(prev. unreleased version), Pretty Persuasion (unrel. live-in-the-studio version 17/2/83), White Tornado (prev. unrel version), Tighten Up (previously on Bucketfull Of Brains flexi) Moon River (unrel. live-in-the-studio version 17/2/83),

☐ "Fables Of The Reconstruction"	IRS	MC 5592	USA	/85
☐ "Fables Of The Reconstruction"	IRS	DMIRF 1003	UK	4/87
☐ "Fables Of The Reconstruction"				

(MCA mid-price re-issue) IRS DMIRL 1503 UK /87

☐ "Fables Of The Reconstruction"	IRS	CSCS-6082	JAP	/8?
☐ "Fables Of The Reconstruction"				

(CBS mid-price re-issue) IRS/CBS 465380 2 NL /91

☐ "Fables Of The Reconstruction"	IRS	0777 7 13160 2 9	NL	8/92

+ extra tracks: Crazy, Burning Hell, Bandwagon, Driver 8 (live), Maps & Legends (live).

☐ "Life's Rich Pageant"	IRS	MC 5783	USA	7/86
☐ "Life's Rich Pageant"	IRS	DMIRG 1014	UK	12/87
☐ "Life's Rich Pageant"	IRS	CSCS-6083	JAP	/8?
☐ "Life's Rich Pageant"				

(MCA mid-price re-issue) IRS DMIRL 1507 UK /91

☐ "Life's Rich Pageant"

(CBS mid-price re-issue) IRS/CBS 465381 2 NL /91

☐ "Dead Letter Office" + "Chronic Town"
  IRS AM 70054 USA 4/87
☐ "Dead Letter Office" + "Chronic Town"
  IRS CDA 70054 UK 5/87
☐ "Dead Letter Office" + "Chronic Town"

☐	"Dead Letter Office" + "Chronic Town"	IRS	CSCS-6084	JAP	/8?
	(CBS mid-price re.)	IRS/CBS	465382 2	NL	/91
☐	"Document"	IRS	MC 42059	USA	9/87
☐	"Document"	IRS	DMIRG 1025	UK	10/87
☐	"Document"	IRS	320P-842	JAP	/8?
☐	"Document" (MCA mid-price re-issue)	IRS	DMIRL 1508	UK	/91
☐	"Document" (CBS mid-price re-issue)	IRS/CBS	465382 2	NL	/91
☐	"Eponymous"	IRS	MC 6262	USA	10/88
☐	"Eponymous"	IRS	DMIRG 1038	UK	11/88
☐	"Eponymous"	IRS		JAP	/8?
☐	"Eponymous" (CBS mid-price re-issue)	IRS/CBS	465383 2	NL	/91
☐	"Green"	Warner Brothers	WA 25795	USA	11/88
☐	"Green"	Warner Brothers	925 795-2	UK/GE	11/88
☐	"Green"	Warner Brothers	25P2-2389	JAP	/88
☐	"The Collection" (5 CD set in slip box)	IRS	465885.2	NL	8/90

Including:
"Fables Of The Reconstruction" (CDILP 26525)
"Life's Rich Pageant" (CDILP 57064)
"Document" (ILP 460105.2)
"Dead Letter Office" (ILP 450961.2)
"Eponymous" (ILP 4631472)

☐	"Out Of Time" (in US long-box)	Warner Brothers	9-26496-2	USA	3/91
☐	"Out Of Time"				

(special portfolio edition, bound in black board cover with picture CD and 10 postcards)

		Warner Brothers	9-26527-2	USA	3/91
☐	"Out Of Time"	Warner Brothers	7599-26496-2	UK/GE	3/91
☐	"Out Of Time"	Warner Brothers	WPCP-4195	JAPAN	3/91
☐	"The Best Of REM"	IRS	MIRH 1	UK	9/91
☐	"Rapid Ear Movement" (6 CDs in 12" yellow box)	Panther	no number	UK	12/91

(An awful repackaging job by a UK distributor. Includes 5 standard REM CD's plus the "Audio.Visual" interview CD)

☐	"Automatic For The People"	Warner Brothers	9-45055-2	USA	10/92
☐	"Automatic For The People"	Warner Brothers	9362-45055-2	GE	10/92
☐	"Automatic For The People"	Warner Brothers	9-45122-2	USA	10/92

(special limited edition. CD has same musical content as regular CD but lacks the track list usually displayed on the disc itself. CD comes in paper slip cover, packaged in square pine box with sliding cover. Album title, etc, embossed into wood. Complete with special inserts not included in the regular issue).

CASSETTES

Nobody in their right mind collects cassettes, nevertheless we include below some interesting cassette releases. All official REM albums and the "Chronic Town" mini-album are available in cassette format bearing identical track listings to their vinyl equivalent (any deviations from this are listed below). Note that the original cassette issue of "Murmur" was supposed to include the non-album B-side "There She Goes Again" but, although insert cards listing this track were printed, it was never added to the tape. Also of note is the original REM demo cassette, which the band mailed out early in their career to prospective record labels, club owners and the like. According to Peter Buck about 300 were sent out that included the original (Hibtone version) "Radio Free Europe", "White Tornado" (same version as later included on "Dead Letter Office"), a snippet of "Sitting Still" ("done polka style") and half of an un-named surf instrumental. An additional 100 cassettes also contained Mitch Easter's remix "Radio Free Europe (Radio Dub)". The zeroxed cassette covers were hand-coloured by the band.

NOTABLE REM CASSETTES
"Murmur + Reckoning" (2 on 1 cassette)
A&M   AMC 24109   UK   /8?
"Reckoning"
IRS   IRSC 7045   UK   /91
    NOTE: Different cover. Songs on back listed vertically not horizontally.
"Fables Of The Reconstructon"
IRS   MIRFC 1003   UK   /8?
    NOTE: Different cover; all balck with album sleeve on front.
"Dead Letter Office" (promo pre-release cassette)
IRS   CS-70054   USA   /87
"Eponymous" (promo cassette)
IRS   IRS-6262   USA   /88
"New Music Seminar '84" (various artists sampler cassette)
IRS   IRS 40+   USA   /84
    NOTE: includes "Pale Blue Eyes" and "Pretty Persuasion" by R.E.M.

CASSETTE SINGLES
The One I Love/Maps And Legends (live)
IRS   IRSC-53171   USA   9/87
It's The End Of The World As We Know It (And I Feel Fine)/Last Date
IRS   IRSC-53220   USA   1/88
Stand/Memphis Train Blues
Warner Brothers   4-27688   USA   1/89
Pop Song 89/Pop Song 89 (acoustic)
Warner Brothers   4-27640   USA   5/89
Orange Crush/Ghost Riders
Warner Brothers   W2960C   UK   5/89
Get Up/Funtime
Warner Brothers   4-22791   USA   10/89
Stand/Pop Song 89
Warner Brothers   4-21864   USA   /90
    NOTE: Warner brothers 'Backtrax' series
Losing My Religion/Rotary Eleven
Warner Brothers   W0015C   UK   2/91
Shiny Happy People/Forty Second Song
Warner Brothers   W0027C   UK   5/91

Near Wild Heaven/Pop Song 89 (live acoustic version)			
Warner Brothers	W0055C	UK	8/91
The One I Love/Crazy			
IRS	IRMC 178	UK	9/91
Radio Song/Love Is All Around (live)			
Warner Brothers	W0072C	UK	11/91
Radio Song (Tower Of Luv Bug mix)/Love Is All Around (live)			
Warner Brothers	4-40229	USA	11/91
It's The End Of The World As We Know It (And I Feel Fine)/Radio Free Europe (LP version)			
IRS	IRMC 180	UK	12/91
Losing My Religion/Losing My Religion (live acoustic version)			
Warner Brothers	9362-40399-4	GE	/92
Drive/World Leader Pretend			
Warner Brothers	9362-45055-4	GE	9/92

UNOFFICIAL THAI CASSETTES

Pirate copies of official releases widely available in Thailand. The two releases of both "Document" and "Green" have different sleeves, but as a general rule all Thai casettes use the original artwork. The quality is NOT of European standards but better than the Polish postcard releases! The existence of the cassettes listed below is confirmed, but there may well be others. We have no reliable releases dates, so none are given.

"Life's Rich Pageant"	Michael	M642	THAI
"Dead Letter Office"	?	2260	THAI
"Document"	?	2474	THAI
"Document"	Michael	M 1006	THAI
"Eponymous"	Musicals	MSC 993	THAI
"Eponymous"	Michael	1296	THAI
"Green"	Musicals	MSC 1045	THAI
"Green"	Best Eagle	PS 1507	THAI
"Out Of Time"	?	5-2412	THAI

POSTCARD SINGLES

These strange releases originate in Poland - the tracks are pressed directly onto the cardboard postcard. The B+H releases are complete with flimsy paper envelopes with a generic illustration (see example). They look like postcards and, if you risk your stylus attempt to play them.......they sound like postcards! Nevertheless, these odd issues are highly collectable! We have no reliable release dates, so none are given.

Sitting Still	K3 Records	-	POLAND /8?
Femme Fatale	K3 Records	-	POLAND /8?
The One I Love	B+H Records	PUR 000859	POLAND /8?
Fall On Me	B+H Records	PUR 000860	POLAND /8?
Radio Free Europe	B+H Records	PUR 000957	POLAND /8?
So. Central Rain (I'm Sorry)	B+H Records	PUR 000958	POLAND /8?

REM TRACKS INCLUDED ON VARIOUS ARTISTS COMPILATION ALBUMS, 12" EPS AND CDS

REM TRACK(S) **TITLE**
                  LABEL/CATALOGUE NO/COUNTRY/DATE
                  (All titles are albums, unless otherwise noted)

"Gardening At Night"   "A New Optimism"
                              Situation Two SITU 11   UK   12/84
"Windout"   "Bachelor Party" (Film soundtrack)
                              IRS IRSA 7051   UK   12/84
"Windout"   "Bachelor Party" (Film soundtrack)
                              IRS ILP 26138   NL   12/84
"Harborcoat"   "KROQ Presents The Normal Noise Of IRS"
                              IRS 28 AP 2830 (IR)   JAPAN   1984
"Radio Free Europe"   "Just What The Doctor Ordered"
                              IRS ILP 26807   NL   1985
"Radio Free Europe"   "Just What The Doctor Ordered"
                              IRS ILP 26807   ISRAEL   1985
"Can't Get There From Here"   "New Rock Collection" (Promo only)
                              CBS 950.104   BRAZIL   1985
"Ages Of You"   "Live! For Life"
                              IRS IRS 5731   USA   5/86
"Ages Of You"   "Live! For life"
                              IRS MIRF 1013   UK   5/86
"(All I Have To Do Is) Dream" "Athens GA - Inside/Out" (Film soundtrack album)
 & "Swan Swan H"   IRS 6185   USA   1987
"Fall On Me" & "   "The Best Of IRS"
 (All I Have To Do Is) Dream" IRS LSP 980142 1   GREECE   1987
"Radio Free Europe" & "Fall On Me" "Kickin' Back To The Future" (CD)
                              CBS/Sony 32 DP 843   JAPAN   1987
"The One I Love"   "The IRS Singles"
                              IRS MIRL 1501   UK   1988
"Romance"   "Made In Heaven" (Film soundtrack)
                              Elektra 9 60729   USA   1988
"Deck The Halls"   "Winter Warnerland" (Promo only double-LP compilation)
                              Warner Brothers PRO-A-3328 (LP) USA   12/88
                              Warner Brothers PRO-CD-3328 (CD)USA   12/88
"Orange Crush"   "Promo Disco Internacional No.62" (Promo only 12" EP)
                              WEA 6WP 0065   BRAZIL   1988
"Orange Crush"   'WBR New Music Report' (CMJ Music sampler)(Promo CD)
                              Warner Brothers PRO CD 3339   USA   198?
"Stand"   "Promo Disco Internacional No.??" (Promo only 12" EP)
                              WEA   BRAZIL   1989
"Stand"   "Rock Star Special 1" WEA 6WP.1008 BRAZIL 1989
"Stand"   Warner Brothers 4-track promo 12" with title sleeve.
                              REM plus other artists: Karen Knight, Travelling Wilburys, Oingo Boingo.

Song	Release	Country	Date
"Stand"	"Super Stars/Super CD" (Pioneer sampler)(Promo CD)		
	WEA/Pioneer SCD1	USA	1989
	WEA 6WP 1033A	BRAZIL	1989
"It's The End Of The World As We Know It (And I Feel Fine)"	"Greenpeace - Breakthrough" Melodia A60 00439 008	RUSSIA	1989
"It's The End Of The World As We Know It (And I Feel Fine)"	"Greenpeace - Rainbow Warriors" RCA PL 74065	EURO	6/89
"Turn You Inside Out"	"Follow Our Tracks" (Promo only compilation)		
	Warner Brothers PRO-A-3503 (LP)	USA	1989
	Warner Brothers PRO-CD-3503 (CD)	USA	1989
"Superman"	"These People Are Nuts" (compilation CD)		
	IRS IRSD-82010	USA	1989
"Cool It"	"CMJ Presents Certain Damage, Vol.23" (2 CD set)		
	CMJ CD-023/1	USA	1990
	(30 sec. public service announcement for the National Wildlife Federation by Michael Stipe)		
"I Walked With A Zombie"	"Where The Pyramid Meets The Eye (Tribute To Roky Erickson)" (CD)		
	Sire/Warner Brothers WA-2644-22	USA	1990
'Fretless'	"Bis Ans Ende Der Welt" (soundtrack LP/CD)		
	Warner Brothers 7599-26751-1/2	GE	10/91
'Fretless'	"Until The End of The World" (as above, soundtrack CD)		
	Warner Brothers 7599-26707-2	UK	1991
"First We Take Manhattan"	"I'm Your Fan - The Songs Of Leonard Cohen" (Dble LP/CD)		
	East West Records 9031-75598-1/2	UK	9/91
	Columbia 469 0321	NL	1991
'Shiny Happy People'	"Awesome 2" (LP/CD)		
	EMI	UK	10/91
'Shiny Happy People'	"The Greatest Hits of '91" (LP/CD)		
	Star	UK	1991
'Losing My Religion' (live) (recorded at the Capitol Theatre, Charleston, West Virginnia 4/91)	"The Best Of Mountain Stage Vol.2" (CD) Blue Plate Music	USA	1/92

Athens GA - Inside/Out

Where The Pyramid Meets The Eye

Michael Stipe. Photo by Greg Allen.

GUEST APPEARANCES

Robyn Hitchcock & Peter Buck. Photo by Derek Pringle

SESSIONS & GUEST APPEARANCES

PETER BUCK

A long time fan of the UK band The Soft Boys, Peter Buck has often worked in the company of that band's former songwriter/guitarist and vocalist, and now solo artist, Robyn Hitchcock. The first recorded collaboration between Robyn and Peter to appear on vinyl was a demo version of Hitchcock's "Flesh No.1" that was given away on a flexi-disc free with "Bucketfull Of Brains" magazine. A second demo also featuring the duo, and recorded at the same session, "Birds Head" remains unreleased. After this, Buck contributed guitar to a selection of tracks recorded for Robyn's A&M albums, "Globe Of Frogs", "Queen Elvis" and "Perspex Island". During the last few years Robyn Hitchcock has also toured as support to R.E.M., and even joined them onstage playing guitar. Peter Buck has also been known to join Robyn and his band, the Egyptians onstage in both the UK and USA.

In addition to the above, Peter and Robyn have been known to masquerade as "Nigel & The Crosses" (named after the original editor of the aforementioned "Bucketfull Of Brains" magazine) - apart from Buck & Hitchcock, the band's mainstays are Peter Holsapple, Andy Metcalfe and Morris Windsor (the latter pair both ex-Soft Boys and currently with Robyn's Egyptians) although other luminaries like Glenn Tilbrook, Mike Mills and Billy Bragg have also been known to participate. "Nigel & The Crosses" have played at least two gigs - both in 1989 - the first took place at Cubby The Bears club in Chicago, USA, and the second at The Borderline, in London's Charing Cross Road. Two tracks recorded at the second gig ("The Queen Of Eyes" and "Purple Haze") were given away on a 7" single with "Bucketfull Of Brains" magazine (Issue 34) in 1990. The gigs usually feature a bunch of Hitchcock and Soft Boys classics plus covers of songs by 60's icons like the Beatles, The Byrds, and the Kinks, together with chestnuts like "Route 66".

The only Nigel & The Crosses studio recording to be issued to date is a version of the Byrds' "Wild Mountain Thyme" which appears on the Byrds tribute compilation "Time Between" on Imaginary Records. A version of the Bob Dylan classic "Mr. Tambourine Man" was recorded at the same session but remains unreleased.

ROBYN HITCHCOCK & PETER BUCK
"Flesh No.1" (demo version)/SOFT BOYS: Deck
  Of Cards (live) (7" flexi-disc)   Bucketfull Of Brains BOB.17   UK   1987
(Peter accompanies Robyn Hitchcock on guitar. The Soft Boys track also features a more youthful Robyn... but not Peter, of course).

ROBYN HITCHCOCK (& THE EGYPTIANS)
"Globe Of Frogs" LP   A&M AMA 5182   UK   1988
"Globe Of Frogs" LP   A&M SP 5182   USA   1988
(Peter plays 12 string guitar on "Chinese Bones" & "Flesh Number One (Beatle Dennis)"
Flesh No.1/Legalized Murder (promo 12")   A&M SP 17549   USA   1988
(Peter plays guitar on "Flesh No.1")

Balloon Man/A Globe Of Frogs (electric)(7")   A&M AM 13023   USA   1988
Balloon Man/A Globe Of Frogs (electric)(promo 12") A&M SP-17530   USA   1988.
(Peter plays guitar on an electric version of the track "Globe Of Frogs")
"Queen Elvis" LP   A&M 5241   USA   1989
"Queen Elvis" CD   A&M CD 5241   USA   1989
(Peter plays guitar on "Madonna Of The Wasps", "Wax Doll", "Swirling" and "Freeze")
Madonna Of The Wasps/One Long Pair Of Eyes
  (acoustic)/More Than This (Promo only CD)   A&M CD 17718   USA   1989
Madonna Of The Wasps/One Long Pair Of Eyes
  (acoustic)/More Than This (12")   A&M SP 17697   USA   1989
(Peter plays guitar on "Madonna Of The Wasps" -same version as LP/CD)
One Long Pair Of Eyes (edit)/The Ghost In You
  (live)/Freeze (Shatter mix) (promo 12")   A&M SP 17729   USA   1989
(NB: in addition to the tracks mentioned above we also assume that Peter Buck plays on "Freeze (Shatter Mix)" one of the two extra cuts on the CD)

Peter Buck appeared live with Robyn Hitchcock in Athens, GA, USA on 25/3/88 - a live recording of the gig was broadcast on local FM radio.

NIGEL & THE CROSSES (INCLUDING ROBYN HITCHCOCK & PETER BUCK)

"Time Between - A Tribute To The Byrds" (LP/CD) Imaginary ILL CD 400   UK   1989
(one track only: "Wild Mountain Thyme")
"Wild Mountain Thyme" (DJ only one-sided 7")   (white label)   USA 1989
The Queen Of Eyes/Purple Haze (live) (7" single) Bucketfull Of Brains BOB.28 UK 1990

Of course, when he's not working with Robyn Hitchcock, Peter Buck keeps his hand in by playing with, or producing a host of other artists. These occurances are listed in chronological order as far as possible.

REPLACEMENTS

"Let It Be" (LP)   Zippo ZONG 002   UK   1984
"Let It Be" (LP)   Twin Tone TTR 8441 USA   1984
I Will Dare/20th Century Boy/Hey Good
  Lookin' (live) (12")   Twin Tone TTR 8440 USA   1984
(Buck plays guitar on "I Will Dare" on both the album and 12")

THE DREAM ACADEMY

"Dream Academy" (LP)   Warner Brothers 25265 USA   1985
"Dream Academy" (LP)   Blanco Y Negro   UK   1985
(Peter Buck plays guitar on "The Party". The recording sessions took place at the home of Dave Gilmour - Pink Floyd - and it has been suggested that perhaps Peter took on the session just so that he could have a gander at the place!)

THE FLESHTONES

"Speed Connection II" (live LP)   IRS IRS 5627   USA   1985
"Speed Connection II" (live LP)   IRS ILP 26412   UK   1985
(Peter Buck plays guitar on "When The Night Falls" and the REM song "Wind Out" recorded live at the Gibus club, Paris, France 4/3/85. Oddly, Buck only appears on "Wind Out" on the USA version of the LP, as the UK issue substitutes a different take of the same song!)
"The Fleshtones Presents: Time Bomb. The Big
  Bang Theory" (LP)   Skyclad (bare)FLESH.3, USA   1988
"The Fleshtones Presents: Time Bomb. The Big
  Bang Theory" (LP)   New Rose ROSE 137   FR   1988
(above album includes the Fulltime Men track "High On Drugs" with Peter on guitar)

DREAMS SO REAL
Everywhere Girl/Whirl (7") Coyote TTC 8556 USA 1985
"Father's House" (LP) Coyote TTC 8688 USA 1986
(Both above records by Athens, GA band, produced by Peter Buck)

WOOFING COOKIES
In The City/VB Side (7") Midnight MID 4512 USA 1986
(A-side of the above produced by Peter Buck)
"Hanging Out At Midnight" (compilation LP) Midnight MIRLP 127 USA 1986
(According to the sleevenote, the Woofing Cookies track included on the above, "Girl Next Door" was "produced by Peter Buck of REM")

THE FEELIES
"The Good Earth" (LP) Coyote TTC 8673 USA 1986
"No One Knows" (12" EP) Coyote TTC 8695 USA 1986
"No One Knows" (12" EP) Rough Trade RTT 180 UK 1986
(The whole "Good Earth" LP was co-produced by Peter Buck, Glen Mercer and Bill Million. Two tracks from the LP, "The High Road" and "Slipping Into Something" are also featured on the "No One Knows" EP together with versions of "Sedan Delivery" & "She Said, She Said", although neither of these were produced by Peter Buck)

THE FULLTIME MEN
One of Peter Buck's other continuing collaborations is with the Fleshtones' guitarist Keith Streng. With others, these two have formed the occasional band The Full time Men. To date, though, just the records shown below have been released.
I Got Wheels/One More Time/Way Down South (12") Coyote TTC 8562 USA 1986
I Got Wheels/One More Time/Way Down South (12") What Goes On UK 1986
(Peter Buck plays guitars and banjo and co-produced the above, which also features Mike Mills playing organ on "One More Time")
"Your Face, My Fist" (LP) Coyote TTC 88138 USA 1988
(Peter Buck plays on the tracks: "I Got Wheels" & "High On Drugs". The phrase "High On Drugs" is reputed to be the original title for the "Fables Of The Reconstruction" LP - unfortunately, IRS weren't having any of it!)

THE UPBEATS
"Pop Songs" (LP) Laser LLP 102 USA 1986
(Peter Buck plays guitar on the track "Just Another Pop Song")

BRUCE JOYNER
The World Needs A Little More Love/In Dreams (7") New Rose NEW 114 FR 1987
(Buck plays rhythm guitar on A-side)
"Hot Georgia Nights" (LP) New Rose ROSE 129 FR 1987
(Peter Buck plays guitar on 'the tracks 'The World Needs A Little More Love" and "Melrose Avenue" on the above album)

CHARLIE PICKETT & THE MC3
"In The Wilderness" (LP) Fundamental Music SAVE 066 UK 1988
"In The Wilderness" (LP) Safety Net USA 1988

(Peter Buck produced the album and plays guitar on two tracks, "Death Letter" & "John The Revelator". An excellent hard driving rock'n'roll record - well worth hearing. As an illustration of what a pleasant fellow Peter Buck is.....Charlie Pickett: "We were playing Tuscaloosa, Alabama (1985) the same night REM were playing the big school hall. They told everyone, at the end of their show, to go on down to the club where we were playing because it would be really good. They came down in their tour bus - my guitars had all gone out of tune while we were playing so Peter Buck tuned our guitars constantly and handed them to me! At the end of the show he played a song or two with us. Absolutely so gracious and helpful, they're really something else!".)

TOMMY KEENE

"Based On Happy Times" (LP)   Geffen 759924221   USA   1989
(Peter Buck plays guitar on "Our Car Club" and mandolin on "A Way Out").

DRIVIN'N'CRYIN'

"Mystery Road" (LP)   Island 91226   USA   1989
(Peter Buck plays electric dulcimer. Also notable is the fact that R.E.M. covered the song "With The People" from this LP during the "Green" tour).
"Fly Me Courageous" (10" EP)   Island 10 IS 523   UK   4/92
(Peter produced the track "Toy Never Played With" (demo)).

KEVN KINNEY

"MacDougal Blues" (LP/CD)   Island 791331-1/2   USA   1990
(Kevn is a member of the aforementioned Drivin'n'Cryin', so it's not surprising to find Peter Buck doing production duties on his solo album. Peter Buck has toured with Kevn in 1991 and 1992)

PETER BUCK & NIKKI SUDDEN

"Sun Is Shining" (7" flexi-disc)   Reflex Magazine   USA   1990
(Also playing on the track are Tim Neilsen & Jeff Sullivan from Drivin'n'Cryin'. The disc was produced by Buck & Sudden and given away with the Fall 1990 issue of 'Reflex' magazine)

INDIGO GIRLS

"Nomads Indians Saints" (LP)   Epic 467308 1   EUR   1990
(Peter plays dulcimer on the track "World Falls"),

RUN WESTY RUN

"Hardly Not Even" (LP)   SST 192   USA   1988
(Buck produced LP with Grant Hart)
"Green Cat Island" (LP)   Twintone TTR 89199-1   USA   1990
(Album produced by Peter Buck and Run Westy Run)

CONCRETE BLONDE

"Bloodletting" (LP)   IRS 064-24 1059 1   EUR   1990
(plays guitar and mandolin on track "Darkening Of The Light")

THE DASHBOARD SAVIORS

All Before/Town (7")   Sol SOL-9114-7   USA   1991
(produced both tracks, plays 12-string guitar on B-side)

CHRIS STAMEY

"Fireworks" (CD)   Rhino R2 70766   USA   1991
(Peter plays electic guitar on the track "The Brakeman's Consolation". REM's 'fifth member' Peter Holsapple is featured throughout the album, on backing vocals, piano, 12-string guitar and harmonica).

THE BEATS
"Up Until Now" (CD)　　　　　　　　　　　　　Cottage Records CD COT 102　UK　　　1991
(For contractual reasons Peter is credit with playing on just one track on this CD by the 25-strong collection of musicians from the Athens/Tifton area of Georgia - however his guitar work may well be evident elsewhere. Also involved is John Keane, whose studio is frequently used by REM)

STEVE WYNN
"Dazzling Display"　　　　　　　　　　　　　Rhino R2 70283　　　　　USA　　　1992
(Peter plays 12-string & acoustic guitar on "Tuesday" and "Close Your Eyes", acoustic guitar & mandolin on "A Dazzling Display", acoustic guitar on "Halo" and "As It Should Be").

UNCLE TUPELO
Sauget Wind/Looking For A Way Out/Take My
　Word (7")　　　　　　　　　　　　　　　　Rockville ROCK 6089-7　　USA　　　1992
("Take My Word", recorded at John Keane's studio in Athens in March 1992 was produced by Peter Buck)
"March 16-20, 1992" (CD)　　　　　　　　　Rockville ROCK6090-2　　USA　　　8/92
(Peter is credited with feedback on the track "Wait Up". He also produced the album at John Keane Studios in Athens).

VARIOUS ARTISTS
"Make The City Grovel In It's Dust" (LP)　　　Twilight Records TR 015　USA　　　1987
(produced track "What's Left For Today" by the Shades Of Shame)

Apart from the forgoing, Peter Buck is also reputed, and indeed reported to have undertaken sessions with The Moberlys (last heard of based in the LA area) and The Reaction (from Chicago); a mooted session with songwriter, singer, actor and lunatic Mojo Nixon seems to have come to nothing.....a shame! Nevertheless, Buck has backed Mojo live, on acoustic guitar, on at least one occasion. Due for release in 1993 is an album by Sam Phillips (wife of T-Bone Burnett) featuring Peter Buck.

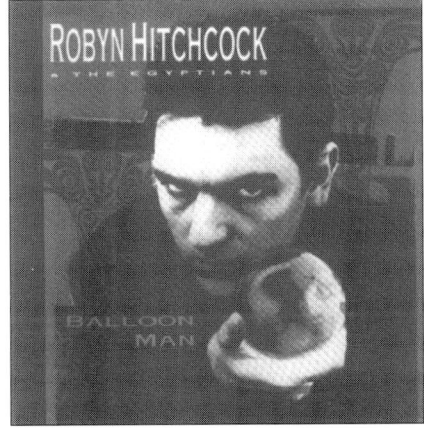

Robyn Hitchcock Balloon Man 7"A&M AM 13023 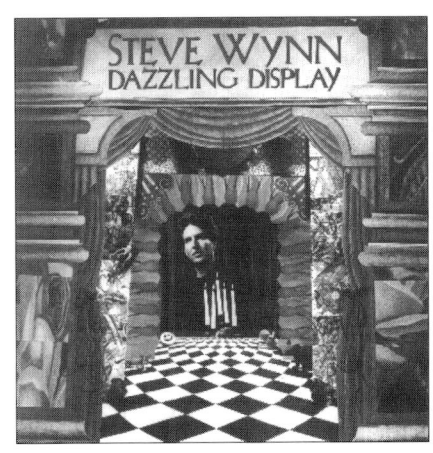　　　　　*Steve Wynn "Dazzling Display"Rhino R2 70283*

MICHAEL STIPE

Whilst not quite as obviously industrious as a guest artiste/producer as Peter Buck, Michael Stipe has also been far from idle when not working directly with REM. Also, a major part of his share time is devoted to his passion for film-making. For several years now Mr. Stipe and Jim McKay have been partners in 'C-00 Filmcore', a venture bent on promoting and making avante garde films for the video market. Amongst other things Stipe co-directed the Henry Rollins Band's "What Am I Doing Here" video and produced the "Fall On Me" video for REM.

On the record front, Michael has kept a beady eye on the Texas Hotel label, operating out of Santa Monica, California - to date he has worked directly with three of the labels roster of artists: Hetch Hetchy, Vic Chestnutt and the Chickasaw Mudd Puppies. His own solo project tentatively entitled "Field Recordings" appears to have been shelved for the moment.

TANZPLAGEN

Live demo (cassette)　　　　　　　　　　no label　　　　　　　　USA　　　1981/2
(Live demo tape - said to be unlistenable - featuring Michael Stipe's experimental noise band, which existed alongside R.E.M. for a short period. A single, apparently featuring a vocal duet between Michael and Lynda Stipe, who went on to form her own Oh Ok! group, was recorded for the Dasht Hopes label during the same period, but remains unreleased).
"Tanzplagen" (LP/CD)　　　　　　　Strange Way 11056　　　　GE　　　1991
(Features Michael Stipe, W.L. Self, David Pierce, Lynda Stipe, Linda Hopper & Neil McArthur. Tracks are: "Treason", "Meeting" - both apparently from a 'lost' single, "Living By The Neck", "Meeting", "Peter Pan" - these last 3 live at the 40 Watt Club in Athens, GA, USA, in 1981).

JASON & THE SCORCHERS

"Fervor" (mini-LP)　　　　　　　　Praxis PR 6654　　　　　　USA　　　1983
"Fervor" (mini-LP)　　　　　　　　EMI America SQ 19008　　USA　　　1984
(Michael Stipe sings harmony vocals on "Hot Nights In Georgia" and co-wrote "Both Sides Of The Line". The original, and now very rare Praxis release was reissued on EMI America in a re-recorded version with one extra track)

THE GOLDEN PALOMINOS

Omaha/I.D. (Like A Version) (7")　　　Celluloid SCEL 56　　　USA　　　1985
Omaha/For A Few Dollars More (12")　Celluloid CEL 183　　　USA　　　1985
(Stipe sings lead on "Omaha" - only - on both of the above releases)
Boy (Go)/The Animal Speaks (7")　　　Celluloid SCEL 58　　　USA　　　1985
Boy (Go)(edited version, 3.48)/Boy (Go)(long version,
5.19)/The Animal Speaks (12" promo)　Celluloid CEL 188　　　USA　　　1985
"Visions Of Excess" (LP)　　　　　　　Celluloid CELL 6118　　USA　　　1985
(Stipe sings lead vocals on "Boy (Go)", "Clustering Train" and "Omaha" and co-wrote the first two of these songs with Anton Fier and Jody Harris; "Omaha" is a version of the Moby Grape classic)
"Trilogy" (Triple LP compilation)　　　Celluloid CELL 80808　USA　　　1985
(The same versions of "Omaha" and "Clustering Train", as above, are featured on this set).
"Drunk With Passion" (CD)　　　　　　Virgin/Venture CDVE 905　USA　　1991
"Drunk With Passion" (CD/LP)　　　　Virgin　　　　　　　　UK　　　1991
(Michael sings on "Alive & Living Now" on the above LP/CD)
Alive & Living Now/same (promo only 7")　Virgin　　　　　SPAIN　　1991
"A History, Vol.1 (1982-1985)" (CD)　　Restless 7 72651-2　　USA　　　1992

"A History, Vol.1 (1982-1985)" (CD)　　　　Mau Mau MAUCD 625　　UK　　1992
(includes all but one track of the 'Visions Of Excess' album and thus features Michael on "Boy (Go)", "Clustering Train" and "Omaha").

COMMUNITY TROLLS
"Don't Shoot" (advance promo cassette only)　　Zippo ZONG 009　　UK　　1986
(Advance cassettes of the "Don't Shoot" various artists compilation feature 3 tracks that didn't appear on the final LP. The Community Trolls' track "Tainted Obligations" is one of these 3 missing tracks and features Michael Stipe on lead vocals!)

OFB (AKA OUR FAVOURITE BAND)
"Saturday Nights....Sunday Mornings"(LP)　　Praxis/BT 6041-1-B　　USA　　1987
(Amongst the miriad guests on this LP, Michael Stipe contributes vocals on one track, "Dreamin' Of Eternity", alongside Jason Ringenberg, of Jason & The Scorchers and solo artist Steve Forbert).

HUGO LARGO
"Drum" (LP)　　　　　　　　　　　　　　Relativity 88561-8167-1　　USA　　1987
(Stipe co-produced 3 of the 6 songs on the album, with the band and also contributes instrumentally. The band's Timothy Sommer and Michael Stipe had become friends several years earlier, when the former, then a DJ, interviewed the latter for his radio show on WNYU)
"Drum" (LP)　　　　　　　　　　　　　　Land 002　　　　　　　　UK　　1987
(includes extra track "Harpers", co-written by Michael Stipe)

10,000 MANIACS
"In My Tribe" (LP)　　　　　　　　　　　Elektra 960738　　　　　USA　　1987
"In My Tribe" (LP)　　　　　　　　　　　Elektra EKT 41　　　　　UK　　1987
Like The Weather/A Campfire Song (7")　　Elektra EKR77　　　　　UK　　1987
Like The Weather/A Campfire Song/Poison In The
Well (live)/Verdi Cries (live) (12")　　　　Elektra EKR 77T　　　　UK　　1987
(Michael Stipe sings a duet with his good friend Natalie Merchant on "A Campfire Song" on all the above releases)

HETCH HETCHY
"Make Djibouti" (mini-LP)　　　　　　　Texas Hotel 7　　　　　USA　　1988
(Produced by Michael Stipe. The credits list one 'Michael Meister' on backing vocals & 'muscle relaxant'.....sounds suspicious, but Michael Meister is, in fact, the man behind the Texas Hotel label. Hetch Hetchy - named after a valley in the Yosemite National Park - include Lynda Limner (aka Stipe, Michael's sister, formerly with Oh Ok) in their ranks)

VARIOUS ARTISTS
"Stay Awake" (LP)　　　　　　　　　　　A&M SP3918　　　　　USA/UK　　1988
(Michael Stipe sings on the track "Little April Shower" accompanied by Natalie Merchant, Mark Bingham and The Roches. The record is a Walt Disney tribute album, by the way)

"Make The City Grovel In It's Dust" (LP)　　Twilight Records TR 015　　USA　　1987
(a compilation featuring a track called "Friends", co-produced by Michael with the band Die Monster Die).

"Hard Cell" (CD)　　　　　　　　　　　Mau Mau MAUCD 622　　UK　　1992
(A compilation of material on the Celluloid label, which features the Golden Palominos recording of "Omaha" with Mr. Stipe on vocals).

SYD STRAW
"Surprise" (LP)　　　　　　　　　　　　Virgin 91266　　　　　　USA　　1989
Future 40's (String Of Pearls)/Taken (7")　　Virgin VUS 6　　　　　UK　　1989

Michael Stipe

Future 40's (String Of Pearls)/Taken/Learning The Game (12") Virgin VUST6 UK 1989
Future 40's (String Of Pearls)/Taken/Learning The Game (3" CD single) Virgin VUSCD6 UK 1989
(Michael Stipe co-wrote the track "Future 40's (String Of Pearls)" with Syd and sings with her on it. "Taken" is a Peter Holsapple song, trivia fans!)

VIC CHESTNUTT
"Little" (LP/CD) Texas Hotel 20/20CD USA 1990
(LP produced by Michael Stipe who possibly sings some backing vocals)(A great record by a Texas singer-songwriter who comes over like a cross between Roky Erickson & Bob Dylan!)

INDIGO GIRLS
"Live At The Uptown College" (video) CBS/CMV Ents 01-049029-81 USA 1990
(Michael sings guest vocals on the track "Kid Fears")
"Tame Yourself" (compilation CD) Warner Brothers 9031-74745-2 UK 1991
(This time he sings on the track "I'll Give You My Skin")

BLUE AEROPLANES
"Swagger" (LP) Ensign CHEN 13 UK 1990
(Michael sings backing vocals on the track "What It Is")

CHICKASAW MUDD PUPPIES
"White Dirt" (mini-LP) Texas Hotel 843 2171 USA 1990
(The Mudd Puppies are a duo, Brant Slay and Ben Reynolds - both old friends of Michael Stipe from his university days. Their forte is raw blues employing a diversity of instrumentation, sometimes home made. Michael co-produced the "White Dirt" EP.)
"Do You Remember" (12" promo) Wing/Mercury PRO 912 USA 1991
(includes interview from October 1990 featuring Michael Stipe)
"8-Track Stomp" (CD) Wing/Polydor 843 936-2 UK/USA 1991
(Produced by Michael Stipe with Willie Dixon. Stipe sings backing vocals, plays keyboards, tambourine, tuba and handclaps on the following tracks: "Superior", "Night Time (Ain't Got No Eyes)", "Wasp", "Cold Blue", "Omaha", "Do You Remember" and "Words & Knives" which he co-wrote.)

THE DAISY GROUP
The Hum Of Life/My Body Is Falling Apart (7") Planned Obsolescence PO2 USA 1991
(Michael produced this record by a local Athens band)

MAGNAPOP
"Maganapop" (CD) Play It Again Sam BIAS 220CD BELGIUM 1992
(Michael produced 4 of the 9 tracks: "Chemical", "Favourite Writer", "Complicated" and "Merry").
If only to stop people pointing this out, please also note that Mr. Stipe took the photos that grace the labels of the following records:

OH-OK
"Furthermore What" (mini-LP) DB Records DB69 USA 1983
(The group features one Linda Limner - nee Stipe)

DOWNY MILDEW
"Broomtree" (LP) Texas Hotel 4 USA 1987

As to future releases, a Stipe co-composition, on which he sings, entitled "Trout", will be included on the Neneh Cherry album "Home Brew" due for release on Virgin. Michael has also recorded a cover of Robyn Hitchcock's "Arms Of Love", with the Athens band Asa Nisi Masa, destined for a benefit album.

MIKE MILLS

Judging by the meagre pickings below, it might be assumed that when not gainfully employed touring the world and making records with REM, messrs Mills and Berry are lazy, indolent and withdrawn.....but we are sure that this cannot be the case! In mitigation, we should mention here that Mike & Bill have been know to play as part of The Corn Cob Webs - a five-piece reputedly indulging themselves in Al Green and Led Zeppelin covers, also featuring Gevin Lindsay, Wade Hestor and Paul Edwards.

Mike & Bill also played together, prior to the formation of REM, in bands know as Shadowfax and The Back Door Band - a live tape of the latter, presumably recorded in the late 1970's, is reputed to exist and has been described by Peter Buck as "the worst thing you've ever heard".

KILKENNY CATS
"Hands Down" (LP)　　　　　　　　Coyote TTC 8670　　　　USA　　1986
(Album produced by Mike Mills. Not a great record in our humble opinion, although the band's earlier B-side "Of Talk" is well recommended)

THE FULLTIME MEN
I Got Wheels/One More Time/Way Down
　South (12")　　　　　　　　　　　Coyote TTC 8562　　　　USA　　1986
I Got Wheels/One More Time/Way Down
　South (12")　　　　　　　　　　　Shigaku SHIG 1T　　　　UK　　 1986
(Mike plays organ on 'One More Time')

WAXING POETICS
"Hermitage" (LP)　　　　　　　　　Emergo EM 9610　　　　 USA　　1987
(Album co-produced by Mike Mills and Mitch Easter. Mike plays piano on the song "Return")

BILLY JAMES
"Sixes & Sevens" (LP)　　　　　　　Twilight Records TR 016　USA　　1988
(Mike Mills produced the album for this Athens group, and mixed it with John Keane).

KEVN KINNEY
"MacDougal Blues" (LP/CD)　　　　Island 7.91331-1/2　　　 USA　　1990
(whistles on the song "Chico & Maria". Wow!)

ROBBIE ROBERTSON
"Storyville" (CD)　　　　　　　　　Geffen GEFD-24303　　　USA　　1991
(Mike contributes background vocals on the track "Shake This Town")

Mike Mills. Photo by Marty Perez

BILL BERRY

Bill's underwhelming tally of extra-curricular activities have been noted already, so let's not dwell on the subject. Apart from his music with REM, below is the staggering catalogue of his work wiith other musicians over the last decade... disgraceful!

MICHELLE MALONE
"New Experience" (LP)   Illuminous June   USA   1988
(Bill Berry plays drums on the track "Into The Night").

THIRTEEN-ONE-ELEVEN
My Bible Is The Latest TV Guide/Things I'd
    Like To Say (12")   Dog Gone DOG 13111   USA   1990
(Yup, it's the solo single alright! Bill goes Country......yee haw!).

COLLABORATIONS INVOLVING MULTIPLE MEMBERS OF R.E.M.

THE SPONGETONES
"Torn Apart" (mini-LP)   Ripete 2154   USA   1984
(The back sleeve of this LP by the long-running North Carolina-based Merseybeat specialists reads: "Special thanks to Don Dixon, Mitch Easter, Mario Cartelli and all of R.E.M. for hand claps on 'Shock Therapy'". Need we say more?)

HINDU LOVE GODS
Gonna Have A Good Time Tonight/Narrator (7")   IRS IRS-52867   USA   1986
Gonna Have A Good Time Tonight/Narrator
    (white label 7")   IRS IRS-52867   USA   1986
"Hindu Love Gods" (LP/CD)   Giant 24406-1/-2   USA   1990
"Hindu Love Gods" (LP/CD)   Giant 7599-24406-1/2   UK   1990
Raspberry Beret/Wang Dang Doodle (7")   WEA W9502   UK   1990
Raspberry Beret/Wang Dang Doodle/Mannish
    Boy (12")   WEA W9502T   UK   1990
Raspberry Beret (1-track promo CD)   Warner Brothers PRO-CD-4414 USA   1990

(The "Gonna Have A Good Time Tonight" single features:Mike Mills, Bill Berry and Peter Buck together with Bryan Cook and Warren Zevon. The front cover of the picture sleeve is by Bill Berry. The recording was originally made at John Keane Studio, Athens, GA in 1984. The band have been known to play live gigs and at least one soundboard quality tape with Bryan Cook on lead vocals is known to exist. The full Hindu Love Gods album, and the singles from it,consisting mainly of cover versions, including "Battleship Chains" and Prince's "Raspberry Beret", displays a new-found fondness for the Blues and features the three REMsters mentioned above plus Warren Zevon, with Bryan Cook missing from the scene this time)..

WARREN ZEVON
"Sentimental Hygiene" (LP)   Virgin 7.90603-1   USA   1987
Sentimental Hygiene/The Factory/Leave My
    Monkey Alone (12")   Virgin VS 995-12   UK   8/87
Sentimental Hygiene/The Factory (7')   Virgin VS 995   UK   8/87

Bill Berry. Photo by Derek Pringle

Bad Karma/Boom Boom Mancini/Leave My Monkey Alone (12″)	Virgin VST 1021	UK	11/87
Bad Karma/Boom-Boom Mancini (7″)	Virgin VS 1021	UK	11/87
Reconsider Me/The Factory/Bad Karma (12″)	Virgin VST 1055	UK	2/88
Reconsider Me/The Factory (7″)	Virgin VS 1055	UK	2/88
Splendid Isolation/Even A Dog Can Shake Hands/ Bad Karma/Gridlock (12″)	Virgin VUST 9	UK	1989
Splendid Isolation/Even A Dog Can Shake Hands (7″)	Virgin VUS 9	UK	1989

(Of all the songs, including those on the "Sentimental Hygiene" LP itself: PETER BUCK plays guitar and BILL BERRY plays drums on "Sentimental Hygiene", "Boom Boom Mancini", "The Factory", "Trouble Waiting To Happen", "Detox Mansion", "Bad Karma", "Even A Dog Can Shake Hands" & "The Heartache". MIKE MILLS plays bass on the same tracks, except "Sentimental Hygiene" & "The Heartache". MICHAEL STIPE sings backup vocals on "Bad Karma". Berry, Buck and Mills co-wrote "Even A Dog Can Shake Hands" with Zevon. Warren Zevon's subsequent album, "Transverse City" features nobody at all from R.E.M., instead there's the likes of 'elder-statesmen' Jerry Garcia, Jack Casady and Neil Young....ho hum!).

INDIGO GIRLS

"Indigo Girls" (LP)	Epic 45044	USA	1989
"Indigo Girls" (LP)	CBS 4634911	UK	1989

(Michael Stipe sings backing vocals on the track "Kid Fears"; Peter Buck, Mike Mills and Bill Berry all play on "Tried To Be True")

THE CYNICS

Way It's Gonna Be/Roadrunner (7″)	Get Hip GH-120	USA	1990

(At the end of this live recording a voice says "Pete Buck & Mike Mills from REM, thanks for coming". Maybe they played on it, or maybe not. Either way the Cynics get themselves free publicity here! Well done lads)

ROBYN HITCHCOCK & THE EGYPTIANS

"Perspex Island" (LP/CD)	A&M7502-15368-1/2	USA	1991
"Perspex Island" (LP/CD)	Go! Discs 7502-15368-1/2	UK	8/91
So You Think You're In Love/Watch Your Intelligence (7″)	Go! Discs GOD 65	UK	1992
So You Think You're In Love/Dark Green Energy/ Watch Your Intelligence (12″)	Go! Discs GODX 65	UK	1992
Oceanside (1 track promo CD)	A&M 75021 7297 2	USA	1991
Ultra Unbelieveable Love/Dark Green Energy (promo CD)	A&M 75021 7273 2	USA	1991
Oceanside/Fair Play (live)/Linden Arden Stole The Highlights (live)/One Long Pair Of Eyes (live) (promo only 12″)	A&M 75021 7300 1	USA	1991

(Michael Stipe sings on 'She Doesn't Exist' and 'Dark Green Energy'. Peter Buck plays on 'Lysander', 'So You Think You're In Love', 'Child Of The Universe', 'Earthly Paradise', 'Oceanside', 'She Doesn't Exist', 'Vegetation & Dimes', 'Ride').

BILLY BRAGG

"Don't Try This At Home" (LP/CD)	Go! Discs	UK	1991
You Woke Up My Neighbourhood/Ontario Quebec & Me (7″)	Go! Discs GOD 60	UK	8/91
You Woke Up My Neighbourhood/Ontario Quebec & Me/Bread & Circuses/Heart Like A Wheel (12″)	Go! Discs GODX 60	UK	8/91

(Michael Stipe sings and Peter Buck plays mandolin and acoustic guitar on "You Woke Up My Neighbourhood").

Michael Stipe & Peter Buck. Photo by Derek Pringle

NIKKI SUDDEN
I Belong To You/Alley Of The Street/
   Jigsaw Blues (CD)   UFO 45003 CD   UK   1991
"The Jewel Thief" (LP/CD)   UFO 4   UK   1991
(Peter Buck, Mike Mills and Bill Berry all feature on the above tracks)

DASHBOARD SAVIOURS
"Kitty" (CD)   MCR 89223   USA   1991
(Peter Buck plays 12-string guitar on the tracks "Town", "Drivin' Blind" and "Dropping". Mike Mills plays organ on "Drivin' Blind" and "Consummation").

THE TROGGS
Don't You Know/Nowhere Road (7")	Essential Recs. ESS 2014	UK	2/92
Don't You Know/Nowhere Road (12")	Essential Recs. ESS T 2014	UK	2/92
Don't You Know/Nowhere Road (CD)	Essential Recs ESS X 2014	UK	2/92
"Athens Andover" (LP/CD)	Essential Recs. ESS LP/CD 180	UK	3/92
Together/Crazy Ann/Turned Into Love (12")	Essential Recs. ESS T2016	UK	5/92
Together/Crazy Ann/Turned Into Love (CD)	Essential Recs. ESS X2016	UK	5/92

(Peter Buck, Mike Mills and Bill Berry play on all the tracks and wrote "Nowhere Road" with Peter Holsapple).

PETER HOLSAPPLE

Peter Holsapple played keyboards and guitar with R.E.M. on the "Green" world-tour. In the pursuance of utter completeness, and because he's such a charming fellow, we'll list his releases here (for all his years in the business, there's only a handful). As of mid-1992, it is understood that mr. Holsapple is no longer in the employ of REM - a shame! He has also recorded numerous records with his excellent band the dB's - a combo highly recommended by R.E.M. and one which all R.E.M. fans should sample. Unfortunately, it must be noted that the dB's have disbanded, although Mr. Holsapple and his ex-associates forge ahead with their own solo business........

PETER HOLSAPPLE
Big Black Truck/Death Garage/
   96 Second Blowout (7")   Car Records CRR 5   USA   1978
"Luxury Condos Coming To Your Neigborhood"
   (ompilation LP - Holsapple appears as 'Mr. Bonus' and performs his death-rock classic
   "Elvis, What Happened?").   Coyote TTC 8559   USA   1985
"Live, Melbourne, 1989" (cassette only)   Fast Fictions FAST.001   AU   1989
(the tracks on the above cassette were recorded on a day off during the Australian leg of REM's "Green" world tour).

PETER HOLSAPPLE & CHRIS STAMEY
"Mavericks" (CD)   Rhino R2 70795   USA   1991
"Mavericks" (CD)   Special Delivery SPDCD1042   UK   6/91

BOOTLEGS

7" BOOTLEGS

☐ "FABLES OF REM"
(no label) REM-01

SIDE 1: Pretty Persuasion,
Radio Free Europe
SIDE 2: West Of The Fields,
(Don't Go Back To) Rockville.
RECORDING DETAILS: Live at Rock City, Nottingham, UK 21/11/84.
COMMENTS: Cover says "Live In Nottingham USA 1986", but actually taken from BBC radio broadcast in 1984 as above.

☐ "LIVE IN CHICAGO"
Top De Luxe 150 302

SIDE 1: Harborcoat (label/cover says "South Central Rain")
SIDE 2: Pale Blue Eyes.
RECORDING DETAILS: Live at the Aragon Ballroom, Chicago, Illinois 7/7/84.
COMMENTS: FM radio broadcast on WXRT. Black and white sleeve.

BOOTLEG ALBUMS

☐ "ACCOUSTIC '87"
(Alpine Records MAC-01)

SIDE 1: The One I Love, Welcome To The Occupation, Disturbance At The Heron House, Finest Worksong, Maps & Legends, Walk Don't Run (Baby Please Don't Go), 1,000,000 Miles Away, Trains.
SIDE 2: The One I Love, Spooky, Disturbance At The Heron House, Finest Worksong, Fever, So. Central Rain, Medley: Leaving On A Jet Plane (with Natalie Merchant)

RECORDING DETAILS: Live at McCabe's Guitar Shop, Santa Monica, CA, USA, 24th May 1987.

☐ "ARCHIVAL FOOTAGE '82 - '89"
(no label)
SIDE 1: Untitled #1, Untitled #2, Untitled #3, Untitled #4, Gardening At Night
SIDE 2: King of Birds, Summertime, Feeling Gravity's Pull, Dark Globe, 9-9, Carnival Of Sorts.

RECORDING DETAILS: Side 1: Tracks 1-4 "Green" sessions. Track 5 live September 1984. Side 2: Track 1 "Pageant" sessions. Tracks 2 and 4 live April 1989. Track 3 live 1985. Track 5 live September 1984. Track 6 live 1982.
COMMENTS: Sessions - good quality. Live 1989 - good audience recordings. Other live - excellent audience recordings. Great black & white sleeve.

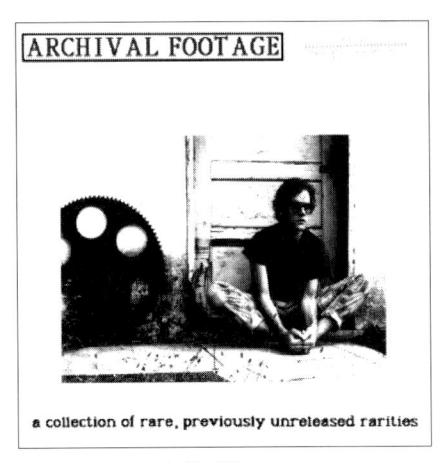

Archival Footage

Bingo Hand Job: The Borderline Club 15/3/91

☐ "BINGO HAND JOB: THE BORDERLINE CLUB 15.3.91"
(Religious Records)(Double LP)

SIDE 1: World Leader Pretend, Half a World Away, Fretless, The One I Love, Hello In There.
SIDE 2: My Eldest Son, Dallas, Disturbance At The Heron House, Belong, Low.
SIDE 3: Love Is All Around, Radio Song, Pop Song 89, Losing My Religion, Fall On Me.
SIDE 4: Stipe at organ (jam), Tom's Diner, Listening To The Higsons, You Ain't Going Nowhere, Get Up, Moon River.

RECORDING DETAILS: The Borderline, London, 15/3/91
COMMENTS: Deluxe colour sleeve. Very good quality.

☐ "BLUE"
(No label. SPLIFF 001)(Double LP)

SIDE 1: Moral Kiosk, Driver 8, Catapult, Hyena, Camera
SIDE 2: Pilgrimage, Talk About The Passion, 7 Chinese Brothers, So. Central Rain (I'm Sorry), Pretty Persuasion
SIDE 3: 9-9, Wind Out, Old Man Kensey, Radio Free Europe, Little America, Burning Down, Pale Blue Eyes, 1,000,000.
SIDE 4: So You Wanna Be A Rock'n'Roll Star/Carnival Of Sorts (Boxcars), Skank.

RECORDING DETAILS: live at the Seattle Music Hall, Seattle, Washington 27th June 1984.
COMMENTS: Excellent soundboard recording but mastered a fraction slow.

☐ "BODY COUNT AT TYRONE'S"
(Brigand Records BRIG 007)

SIDE 1: Just A Touch, A Girl Like You, Dangerous Times, There She Goes Again, I Can Only Give You Everything, I Don't Want You Anymore/All The Right Friends, (Don't Go Back To) Rockville, Body Count.
SIDE 2: Hippy Hippy Shake, Action, Narrator (Jacques Cousteau), She's Such A Pretty Girl, Gardening At Night, Lisa Says, Mystery To Me, Stepping Stone, Permanent Vacation.

RECORDING DETAILS: Live at Tyrone's, Athens, GA, USA 4/10/80.
COMMENTS: Great colour sleeve. Soundboard.

☐ "CAN'T GET THERE FROM HERE"
(Kaxy Recordings KAXY 002)(Double LP)

SIDE 1: Feeling Gravity's Pull, Harborcoat, Green Grow The Rushes, Maps And Legends, Pilgrimage.
SIDE 2: Driver 8, Sitting Still, Good Advices, So. Central Rain (I'm Sorry), Have You Ever Seen The Rain, Can't Get There From Here.
SIDE 3: Seven Chinese Brothers, Auctioneer (Another Engine), Old Man Kensey, Pretty Persuasion, Life And How To Live It, Second Guessing.
SIDE 4: (Don't Go Back To) Rockville, Toys In The Attic, Radar Love, Burning Hell, Talk About The Passion, Little America.

RECORDING DETAILS: Live at Hammersmith Palais, London 28/10/85.
COMMENTS: Good audience recording.

☐ "CHRONIC MURMURINGS"
(Toasted Records 1905)(Double LP)

SIDE 1: Dangerous Times, I Don't Want You Anymore (All The Right Friends), Different Girl, Narrator, Just A Touch, Baby I, Mystery To Me, Permanent Vacation.
SIDE 2: 1,000,000, Ages Of You, Gardening At Night, Carnival Of Sorts (Boxcars), Stumble.
SIDE 3: Catapult, Wolves Lower, Laughing, Easy Come easy Go (Romance), Shaking Through.
SIDE 4: Carnival Of Sorts (Boxcars), Stumble, Wolves Lower, 1,000,000, Windout, Just A Touch.

RECORDING DETAILS: Side 1: Demos, Athens, GA late 1980. Side 2: IRS Demos, Drive In Studio, Winston Salem, North Carolina, 10/81. Side 3: "Chronic Town" out-takes, Drive In Studio, Winston Salem, North Carolina 10/81. Side 4: as above except tracks 5/6: "Reckoning" outtakes, Reflection Studio, Charlotte, North Carolina 12/83 to 1/84)
COMMENTS: Side 1: Fair soundboard. Sides 2-4 Excellent, soundboard. Great colour cover.

☐ "DO YOU REMEMBER - DEAD GIVEAWAY OFFICE"
(no label, C4 70054)

SIDE 1: Welcome To The Starlight, 20th Century Boy, Pills, Barney Miller Theme, Secret Agent Man, Hootenany, DOA, Omaha.
SIDE 2: I Got You Babe, Moon River, Rave On, So You Want To Be A Rock'n'Roll Star, Pale Blue Eyes, I Can't Control Myself, Crazy, Femme Fatale.

RECORDING DETAILS: Side 1, tracks 1 to 6 + Side 2, track 3: live, Tyrones, Athens 1983; Side 1, track 7 + Side 2 tracks 4 to 6 and 8: live, Peppermint Lounge, NY 31/10/83. Side 1, track 8: Golden Palominoes live at the Ritz, NY 9/1/86. Side 2 tracks 1,2 and 7: unknown origin.)
COMMENTS: Tyrones and unknown source recordings excellent soundboard. Peppermint Lounge & Ritz very good audience.

☐ "DOCUMENTARY"
(Toasted Records TRW 1914)(Double LP)

SIDE 1: Finest Worksong, These Days, Welcome To The Occupation, Exhuming McCarthy, Don't Call Me (Orange Crush), Feeling Gravity's Pull.
SIDE 2: King Of Birds, I Believe, Maps And Legends, Driver 8, Superman, Auctioneer (Another Engine).

Bodycount At Tyrone's

Can't Get There From Here

Chronic Murmurings

Do You Remember - Dead Giveaway Office

SIDE 3: Oddfellows Local 151, Earthquake Story (Dialogue), It's The End Of The World As We Know It (And I Feel Fine), Begin The Begin, Strange/Rollers Show (Theme).
SIDE 4: Coyahoga, Fall On Me, Harpers (not listed), The One I Love, Crazy, Eat The Fucking Rich (Pop Song 89), Just A Touch, After Hours.

RECORDING DETAILS: Live circa 1987.
COMMENTS: Good audience recording.

☐ "DOWN SOUTH"
(no label, FTP 0010)

SIDE 1: White Tornado, Shaking Through, (Don't Go Back To) Rockville, Gardening At Night, Sitting Still, Burning Down.
SIDE 2: Chained To The Wall, Ages Of You, Get On Their Way, There She Goes Again, Laughing,

Now That You're Gone (Just A Touch), Radio Free Europe.
RECORDING DETAILS: Side 1, track 1 + Side 2 tracks 1,2, 5 to 7: live circa '82/83; Side 1 tracks 2 to 6 + Side 2 tracks 3 & 4: live Tyrones, Athens 10/1/81).
COMMENTS: Excellent soundboard recordings.

☐ "FINEST LUNCHBOX"
(Toasted Records)

COMMENTS: Boxed set of 7 Toasted label bootleg albums. Includes a unique 92 page book of cuttings, a t-shirt and a postcard.

☐ "FINEST WORKSONGS, DEMOS 1988-1989"
(no label, FWS-8889)

SIDE 1: Finest Worksong, Welcome To The Occupation, Exhuming McCarthy, Disturbance At The Heron House, Pop Song '89, It's The End Of The World As We Know It (And I Feel Fine), Orange Crush.
SIDE 2: Fireplace, Lightnin' Hopkins, I Remember California, Oddfellows Local 151, Get Up, You Are The Everything.

RECORDING DETAILS: Side 1, tracks 5 & 7, and side 2 tracks 3, 5 & 6 are "Green" demos recorded at John Keane Studios, Athens, GA Feb-March 1988. Remaining tracks are "Document" demos recorded at the same studio, Feb- March 1987.
COMMENTS: Excellent soundboard recordings. Black and white cover.

☐ "THE GEORGIA PEACHES - RAPID EYE MOVEMENTS"
(REM Records, L29875)(Double LP)

SIDE 1: Feeling Gravity's Pull, Harborcoat, Driver 8, Pilgrimage, Green Grow The Rushes.
SIDE 2: Sitting Still, Maps And Legends, So. Central rain (I'm Sorry), Laughing, 7 Chinese Brothers.
SIDE 3: Wayward Wind, Can't get There From Here, West Of The Fields, Old Man Kensey, Auctioneer (Another Engine).
SIDE 4: Pretty Persuasion, Little America, Second Guessing, Shaking Through, So You Wanna Be A Rock'n'roll Star, Toys In The Attic.

RECORDING DETAILS: Live at the Bay Front theatre, St. Petersburg, Florida, 26th November 1985.
COMMENTS: Very good audience recording. Good colour sleeve, some issued on pink vinyl. Roger McGuinn guests on "So You Want To Be A Rock'n'Roll Star. Also issued as "Live In St. Petersburg '85" with different black & white deluxe cover.

☐ "GREEN DREAMS"
(Vigotone)(Double LP)

SIDE 1: Pop Song '89, Exhuming McCarthy, Welcome To The Occupation, Disturbance At The Heron House, Turn You Inside Out, Orange Crush.
SIDE 2: Feeling Gravity's Pull, Begin The Begin, Pretty Persuasion, I Believe, Swan Swan H.
SIDE 3: King of Birds (cover says "Flowers Of Guatemala"), Crazy (cover says "Shakin' Through"), Finest Worksong, You Are The Everything, Academy Fight Song.

Documentary

Down South

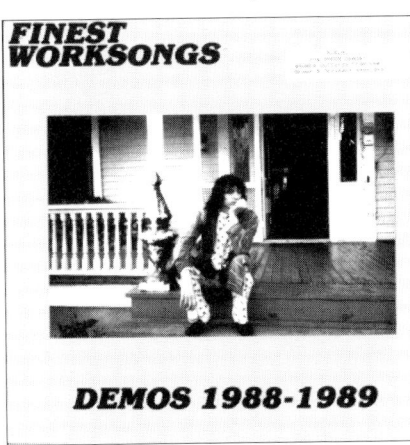

Finest WorksongS, Demos 1988-1989

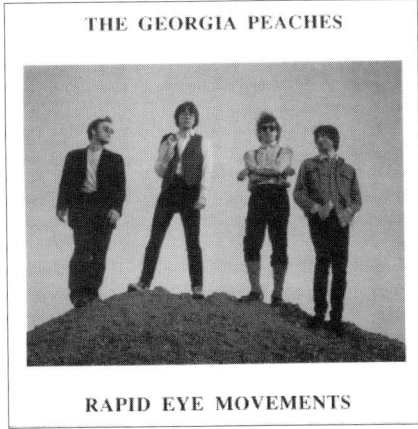

The Georgia peaches - Rapid Eye Movements

SIDE 4: Stand, Perfect Circle, Get Up, It's The End Of The World As We Know It (And I Feel Fine), See No Evil, Academy Fight Song

RECORDING DETAILS: Sides 1, 2, 3 and tracks 1-4 on side 4: Live at the Orlando Arena, Orlando, FL 30th April 1989. Side 4 tracks 5 & 6 from REM Fan Club single.
COMMENTS: FM recording. last two tracks studio.

☐ "HARMONICS IN ETERNITY"
(Rapid Eye Members - no number)

SIDE 1: World Leader Pretend, Fretless, Smiling Faces Sometimes, Tink (Tusk), Loosing My Religion (Losing My Religion), Endgame.
SIDE 2: Jackson, Swan Swan H, Spooky, Falling On Me (Fall On Me), Radio Song, I Enjoy Being A Boy.

RECORDING DETAILS: From a KCRW-FM "Snap" show, Los Angeles, radio broadcast live in the studio 4th March 1991.
COMMENTS: Very good sound, but only average pressing quality.

☐ "L.I.V.E."
(Bandido Records Ltd B006)

SIDE 1: Harlem Nocturne (by The Viscounts), Moral Kiosk, Catapult, Pilgrimage, Return (Seven Chinese Brothers).
SIDE 2: Wolves Lower, Talk About The Passion, Gardening At Night, 9-9 (not listed), West Of The Fields (not listed), Radio Free Europe.

RECORDING DETAILS: Live at the University of Rochester, New York City 18/4/83
COMMENTS: Very good audience recording. Black and white sleeve.

☐ "LIVE IN CHICAGO"
(Me Records 0100)

SIDE 1: Femme Fatale, Radio Free Europe, Gardening At Night, Sitting Still, Pale Blue Eyes, So You Want To Be A Rock'n'Roll Star.
SIDE 2: 9-9, Windout, Driver 8, So. Central Rain (I'm Sorry), Harborcoat, Cushy Tush/Behind Closed Doors, Hyena, Pretty Persuasion.

RECORDING DETAILS: Side 1 tracks 1 to 4 + Side 2: Live at the Aragon Ballroom, Chicago, Illinois 7/7/84. Side 1, tracks 5 & 6: Live at the Capitol Theatre, Passaic, New Jersey 9/6/84
COMMENTS: Picture disc limited to 400 copies (sic). Tracks from Aragon Ballroom are FM broadcast in stereo (WXRT). Remaining tracks taken from "Rock Influences" TV show. Roger McGuinn guests on "So You Want To Be A Rock'n'Roll Star".
ALSO: "Live In Chicago" (Juke Box Records - London XL2) Re-issue of the above but in black vinyl with black and white sleeve.

☐ "MADA MADA (LARRY'S HIDEAWAY 1983 + MORE)"
(Toasted Records 1906)

SIDE 1: Laughing, Pilgrimage, There She Goes Again, Seven Chinese Brothers, Talk About The Passion, Sitting Still
SIDE 2: Harborcoat, Catapult, Gardening At Night, 9-9, Just A Touch, West Of The Fields.
SIDE 3: Radio Free Europe, We Walk, 1,000,000, There She Goes Again, Tighten Up, Don't Want You Anymore (All The Right Friends)
SIDE 4: Easy Come Easy Go (Romance), Million (1,000,000), Pretty Persuasion, Ages Of You, Pilgrimage, Wolves Lower.

RECORDING DETAILS: Side 1, 2 and 3 (tracks 1 to 3): live at Larry's Hideaway, Toronto, Canada 9/7/83. Side 3 tracks 4 to 6 outtakes from Reflection Sound Studios, Charlotte, North Carolina 1/83. Side 4 live at City Gardens, Trenton, New Jersey 16/11/82
COMMENTS: Larry's Hideaway tracks FM broadcast. Reflection Sound Studios demos excellent soundboard. City Gardens from FM broadcast (B-Sharp Concert Series). Great colour sleeve.

☐ "MUMBLE"
(PSA-101)

SIDE 1: Underneath The Bunker, Gardening At Night, 9-9, Windout, White Tornado, Pretty Persuasion, PSA (Bad Day)
SIDE 2: So. Central Rain (I'm Sorry), Swan Swan H, Auctioneer, West Of The Fields, Cuyahoga.

Green Dreams

Harmonics In Eternity

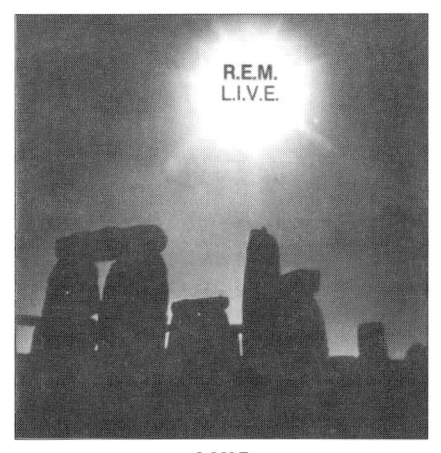

L.I.V.E.

Live In Chicago

Mada Mada

Mumble

RECORDING DETAILS: Side 1 tracks 1 & 2, Side 2 track 5, studio demos 1986. Side 1 tracks 2,3,4 & 6, Side 2 tracks 3 & 4 Rock City, Nottingham 21/11/84. Side 1 track 5, Side 2 tracks 1 & 2: live in the UK.
COMMENTS: Excellent soundboard/FM broadcast.

☐ "NEW ORLEANS - 27/3/89"
(no label)(Double LP)

SIDE 1: Welcome To The Occupation, Disturbance At The Heron House, Turn You Inside Out, Driver 8, (crowd reading screen projections), Orange Crush.
SIDE 2: Cuyahoga, Feeling Gravity's Pull, Time After Time (Annalise), World Leader Pretend.
SIDE 3: I Believe, Pretty Persuasion, Get Up, Auctioneer (Another Engine), It's The End Of The World As We Know It (And I Feel Fine).
SIDE 4: Stand, Fall On Me, You Are The Everything, Finest Worksong, KIng Of Birds.

RECORDING DETAILS: Live at the Lakefront Arena, New Orleans, LA, USA, 27/3/89
COMMENTS: Fair audience recording. Exc. colour sleeve, multi-coloured vinyl.

☐ "NOTTINGHAM"
(Trade Mark Of Quality TMQ 71121)

(Toasted Records 1917)
SIDE 1: Hyena, Talk About The passion, (Don't Go Back To) Rockville, Auctioneer (Another Engine), So. Central Rain (I'm Sorry), Sitting Still, Old Man Kensey.
SIDE 2: Gardening At Night, Nine-NIne (9-9), Windout, Driver 8, Pretty Persuasion, Radio Free Europe.

RECORDING DETAILS: Live at Rock City, Nottingham, UK 21/11/84.
COMMENTS: Taken from BBC Radio broadcast. Some pressed in red vinyl, others in green. Plain green and white sleeve. Also released on Toasted Records (1917)

☐ "PAGEANTRY"
(Pharting Pharoah 13154)(Double LP)

SIDE 1: These Days, Radio Free Europe, Harborcoat, Sitting Still, (The) One I Love, Sharing (Shaking) Through.
SIDE 2: Feeling Gravity's Pull, Last Date, Driver 8, Flowers Of Guatemala, I Believe, Swan Swan H.
SIDE 3: Superman, Can't Get There From Here, Pretty Persuasion, Just A Touch, Fall On Me, Cuyahoga.
SIDE 4: 1,000,000, Strange, All Aboard (Funtime), Life And How To Live It, Begin The Begin, So. Central Rain (I'm Sorry)(Acoustic version)

RECORDING DETAILS: Universal Amptheatre, Los Angeles, CA 30/9/86.
COMMENTS: Fair audience recording. Great colour sleeve. Some copies on pink vinyl, clear vinyl and transparent green vinyl. Also available as a single album.

☐ "PEACE AND LOVE, ANYONE?"
Acme Records ACME 04

SIDE 1: Losing My Religion, Thrash Metal Song, Shiny Happy People, Me And Honey, Endgame.
SIDE 2: Belong, Texarkana, It's A Free World Baby, Here I Am Again, Untitled.

New Orleans

Nottingham

Pageantry

Peace & Love Anyone?

RECORDING DETAILS: Alternate takes, demos from "Out Of Time" sessions.
COMMENTS: Very good qality. NB: The final song listed on the sleeve for each side of the disc does NOT appear on the record. Good full colour sleeve.

☐ "PEASANT DREAMS"
(TMOQ)(Double LP)

SIDE 1: Moral Kiosk, Driver 8, Catapult, Hyena, Camera, Pilgrimage.
SIDE 2: Old Man Kensey, Radio Free Europe, Little America.
SIDE 3: Talk About The Passion, 7 Chinese Brothers, So. Central Rain (I'm Sorry), Pretty Persuasion, Gardening At Night, 9-9.
SIDE 4: Burning Down, Pale Blue Eyes, I Could Live A Million Years (1,000,000).So You Wanna Be A Rock'n'Roll Star, Children From A Smarter Part Of Town (Carnival Of Sorts (Boxcars)), Taking Out The C's (Skank).

RECORDING DETAILS: live at the Seattle Music Hall, Seattle, Washington 27th June 1984.
COMMENTS: very good quality.

☐ "THE POP DREAM"
(Easy Flight Records FLIGHT 801)(Double LP)

SIDE 1: Neverland, Gloria (Tupelo's Tavern, New Orleans, LA 11/6/82), There She Goes Again (Merlyns, Madison, WI 24/4/82), California Dreaming (Warwick University, UK 27/6/85), Toys In The Attic, Radar Love (Hammersmith Palais, London 28/10/85), Paint It Black (Bochum, West Germany 2/10/85), I Can't Control Myself (Bridgeport, CT 13/10/84)
SIDE 2: Radar Love (Hammersmith Palais, London 28/10/85), So You Want To Be A Rock'n'Roll Star (Seattle Music Hall, WA 27/6/84), I Can Only Give You Everything, Secret Agent Man (Barrymore's, Ottawa, Canada 17/8/85), See No Evil (Hammersmith Palais, London 28/10/85), Pills , (I'm Not Your) Stepping Stone (Barrymore's, Ottawa, Canada 17/8/85).
SIDE 3: Have You Ever Seen The Rain (Bochum, West germany 2/10/85), Eight Miles High, Roadrunner (Ripley's, Philadelphia, PA 20/7/83) , In The Year 2525 (Graham Chapel, St. Louis, MO 6/10/84), After Hours (Uinversity Of Amhearts, MA 15/10/84), God Save The Queen, 20th Century Boy (Barrymore's, Ottawa, Canada 17/8/85).
SIDE 4: Smokin' In The Boy's Room (Barrymore's, Ottawa, Canada 17/8/85), Sweet Jane (Kabuki Theatre, San Francisco, CA 10/11/83), Louie Louie (Opheum, Minneapolis 3/7/84), Pale Blue Eyes (WLIR 'In Concert' broadcast), Wild Thing (Queensway Hall, Dunstable, UK 29/11/84), Chicken Train (Graham Chapel, St. Louis, MO 6/10/84), Be Bop A Lula (Markthalle, Hamburg, West Germany 10/10/85).

RECORDING DETAILS: Side 1 track 3, Side 3 tracks 2,3 & 4: soundboard. Side 1 track 6, Side 2 track 2, Side 3 track 1, Side 4 track 4: FM radio broadcasts. Remaining tracks are audience recordings.
COMMENTS: Good colour sleeve.

☐ "POP SONGS '89"
(BMPM-8032)

SIDE 1: Pop Song 89, Get Up, You Are The Everything, King Of Birds, World Leader Pretend, Orange Crush.
SIDE 2: Turn You Inside Out, Hairshirt, I Remember California, Rotary 10, untitled, Perfect Circle.

RECORDING DETAILS: Live 1989 "Green" tour, USA except Side 2 tracks 2 and 5 studio demos 1988.
COMMENTS: Live tracks are very good audience recordings. Demos are excellent soundboard. Black and white cover with insert containing track listing and press article.

☐ "PRETTY PICTURES"
(Easy Flyte Records FLIGHT 130)(Double LP)

SIDE 1: That Beat, All The Right Friends, Tighten Up, There She Goes Again, Moon River, That Beat, Burn It Down (Burning Down).
SIDE 2: Burning Hell, The Lion Sleeps Tonight, Skank, Camera, Second Guessing, Just A Touch, Pale Blue Eyes.
SIDE 3: Catapult, Wolves Lower, Laughing, Easy (Romance), Shaking Through, Carnival Of Sorts (Boxcars), Stumble.
SIDE 4: All The Right Friends, A Different Girl, Narrator, Just a Touch, Baby I, Mystery To Me, Permanent Vacation.

RECORDING DETAILS: Side 1, tracks 1 to 5: 'Murmur' outtakes from Reflection Studios, Charlotte, NC, 1/83. Side 1 tracks 6 & 7 and Side two tracks 1 to 7: demos for 'Reckoning' from Rhythmic Studios, San Francisco, CA, 9/11/83. Side 3: demos for RCA label, recorded at RCA Studio C, New York City, NY, 1-8th February 1982. Side 4: are demos recorded at Tyrones, Athens, GA, late 1980.
COMMENTS: Sides 1 to 3: excellent soundboard; Side 4: Fair soundboard.

The Pop Dream   *Pop Songs 89*

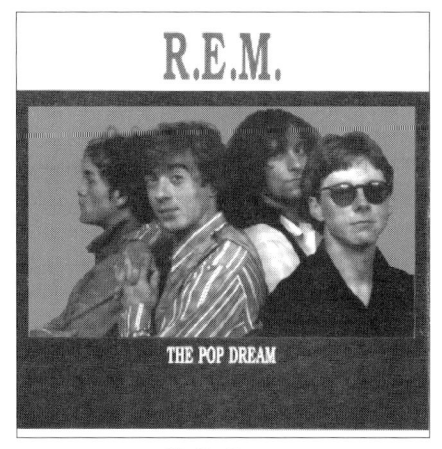

☐ "RADIO FREE GEORGIA"
(Bee Records RM-01)(Double LP)

SIDE 1: Feeling Gravity's Pull, Harborcoat (cover says "Burning Down"), Green Grow The Rushes, 7 Chinese Brothers, Hyena, Good Advices.
SIDE 2: Talk About The Passion, Driver 8, Can't Get There From Here, So. Central rain (I'm Sorry), Maps And Legends, Auctioneer (Another Engine), Old Man Kensey.
SIDE 3: Pretty Persuasion, Life And How To Live It (cover says "Walking In The Streets"), Little America (cover says "Empty Wagon"), Second Guessing, (Don't Go Back To) Rockville,, Just A Touch (cover says "Radio Free Europe").
SIDE 4: Theme From Two Steps Onward (cover says "Don't Be A Stranger"), Gardening At Night, 9-9 (cover says "Conversation"), Wind Out (not listed), Pale Blue Eyes(cover says "Linger On"), Have You Ever Seen The Rain.

RECORDING DETAILS: Live at the Felt Forum, New York, NY 7th November 1986 according to the cover - but probably recorded over a year earlier, around April/May 1985.
COMMENTS: Great concert. Good audience recording. Great colour sleeve - printed both sides.

☐ "REALLY EXCITING MUSIC"
(Easy Flyte Records FLIGHT 201)

SIDE 1: 1,000,000, Ages Of You, Carnival Of Sorts (Boxcars), Shut Down (White Tornado), Radio Free Eurpe, Sitting Still.
SIDE 2: There She Goes Again, Windout, Pretty Persuasion, Time After Time, So. Central rain (I'm Sorry), Little America.

RECORDING DETAILS: Side 1 tracks 1-3 recorded at Drive-In Studio, Winston-Salem, NC 2-7th October 1981. Side 1 tracks 4-6 recorded at Drive-In Studio 15th April 1981 ("Radio Free Europe" is the Jonny Hibbert mix). Side 2, track 1 is 'B' side to "Radio Free Europe" (IRS 9916). Side 2 tracks 2-6 same as normal commercial releases, but before final mixing.
COMMENTS: Side 2 tracks 2-6 are dull; remainder is excellent soundboard quality. Good colour cover.

☐ "RETURN OF THE RICKENBACKER"
(no label)

SIDE 1: Seven Chinese Brothers, Harborcoat, Pretty Persuasion, West Of The Fields, Radio Free Europe, Gloria.
SIDE 2: Ages Of You, We Walk, 1,000,000, There She Goes Again, California Dreaming, Carnival Of Sorts (Boxcars).
RECORDING DETAILS: All tracks from the Paradise Theatre, Boston, MA 13/7/83 except Side 1, track 6 live at Tupelo's Tavern, New Orleans, LA 11/6/82.
COMMENTS: Paradise Theatre tracks are taken from an FM radio broadcast but have been mastered too slow. "Gloria" is a good audience recording. Issued in plain black sleeve.
ALSO ISSUED AS: "Return Of The Rickenbacker(s)" (Kabjdo Records) same as the above but in different black and white sleeve.

☐ "RHYTHMUS ET MELOS"

RECORDING DETAILS: Live at the Music Hall, Seattle, Washington, 27th June 1984.
COMMENTS: single LP

☐ "RIPE! GEORGIA PEACHES"
(Parrot REM-7)(Double LP)

SIDE 1: Rave On, Burning Down, A Girl Like You, Get On Their Way, There She Goes Again, Pretty Persuasion, Body Count
SIDE 2: A different Girl, Action, Narrator, Pretty Girl (Nadine), Baby I, Permanent Vacation.
SIDE 3: Radio Free Europe, Sitting Still, Dangerous Times, I Don't Want You Anymore (All The Right Friends), Shaking Through, Little Girl, (Don't Go Back To) Rockville.
SIDE 4: Windout, Gardening at Night, Wait, Scherezade, Lisa Says, Mystery To Me, (White) Tornado.

RECORDING DETAILS: Live at Tyrone's, Athens, GA 10/1/81
COMMENTS: Excellent soundboard recording. Colour sleeve. Originally issued on pink vinyl.

☐ "ROGER, BILL, MIKE & PETE REMEMBER THE BYRDS"
(The Sons Of Rickenbacker SOR-51188)

SIDE 1: Sunshine Love, The Tears, Chestnut Mare, Tiffany Queen, You Aint Goin' Nowhere, Feel A Whole Lot Better.
SIDE 2: Mr. Spaceman, Bells Of Rhymney, Mr. Tambourine Man, Turn Turn Turn, Eight Miles High, Knockin' On Heavens Door

RECORDING DETAILS: Live in Athens, GA, 11/5/88
COMMENTS: Very good audience recording of Roger McGuinn backed by 'The Southern Gentlemen" aka Bill Berry, Mike Mills and Peter Buck. Also issued as "Byrds Fly South"

☐ "ROLLING STONE"
(Auto Dight Records 1345)(Double LP)

SIDE 1: These Days, Harborcoat, Sitting Still, The One I Love, West Of The Fields, Shaking Through.

Pretty Pictures

Really Exciting Music

Return Of The Rickenbackers

Ripe! Georgia Peaches

SIDE 2: Feeling Gravity's Pull, White Tornado, Flowers Of Guatemala, Maps And Legends, Driver 8.
SIDE 3: I Believe, Seven Chinese Brothers, Instrumental (no title), Superman, Can't Get There From Here.
SIDE 4: Pretty Persuasion, Auctioneer (Another Engine), Little America, Fall On Me, Cuyahoga, 1,000,000.

RECORDING DETAILS: Live at The Syrian Mosque, Pittsburgh, PA 24/10/86.
COMMENTS: Fair audience recording. Colour sleeve using "Rolling Stone" magazine cover.

☐ "SMOKIN' IN THE BOYS ROOM"
(Class Act Records C-116)

SIDE 1: White Tornado, Moral Kiosk, Laughing, There She Goes Again, Talk About The Passion, Sitting Still Harborcoat.
SIDE 2: Smokin' In The Boys Room, 9-9, West Of The Fields, Pretty Persuasion, Carnival Of Sorts (Boxcars), Radio Dub.

RECORDING DETAILS: Side 1, track 1, Side 2 track 6: Drive-In Studios, 7/81. Side 2 track 1 live at the Agora, Hartford, CT 20/7/84. All other tracks live at Larry's Hideaway, Toronto, Canada 9/7/83
COMMENTS: Larry's Hideaway tracks from FM broadcast - excellent sound. "Smokin' In The Boys Room" audience recording. Drive-In Studio tracks: excellent soundboard. Good black and white sleeve.
ALSO ISSUED AS: "Smokin' In The Boys Room". Reissue of the above with different back cover.

☐ "SO MUCH YOUNGER THEN"
(no label FTP-0011)

SIDE 1: Body Count, A Different Girl, Action, Narrator, She's Such A Pretty Girl (Nadine), Baby I, Permanent Vacation.
SIDE 2: Wait, Scherezade, Lisa Says, Mystery To Me, All The Right Friends, Little Girl, Dangerous Times, A Girl Like You.

RECORDING DETAILS: Live At Tyrone's, Athens, GA 10/1/81.
COMMENTS: Excellent soundboard recording. Good red and white sleeve.

☐ "SONGS FOR A GREEN WORLD"
(Flashback World Productions FLASH LP 06.91.0150-33)(Double LP)

SIDE 1: Pop Song '89, Exhuming McCarthy, Welcome To The Occupation, Disturbance At The Heron House, Turn You Inside Out, Orange Crush.
SIDE 2: Feeling Gravity's Pull, Swan Swan H, Begin The Begin, Pretty Persuasion, I Believe.
SIDE 3: King of Birds, Crazy, Finest Worksong, You Are The Everything.
SIDE 4: Academy Fight Song, Stand, Perfect Circle, Get Up, It's The End Of The World As We Know It (And I Feel Fine).

RECORDING DETAILS: Live at the Orlando Arena, Orlando, FL 30th April 1989.
COMMENTS: FM recording. Great gatefold colour sleeve.

☐ "WE'RE BLINKING JUST AS FAST AS WE CAN"
(GLC Great Live Concerts 3791)(Double LP)

SIDE 1: Moral Kiosk, Driver 8 (not listed), Catapult, Hyena, Camera, Pilgrimage.
SIDE 2: Untitled (Old Man Kensey), Radio Free Europe, Little America.
SIDE 3: Talk About The Passion, Seven Chinese Brothers, So. Central Rain (I'm Sorry), Pretty Persuasion, Gardening At Night, 9-9, Windout.
SIDE 4: Burning Down, Pale Blue Eyes, So You Want To Be A Rock'n'Roll Star, Carnival Of Sorts (Boxcars), Skank.

RECORDING DETAILS: Live at the Seattle Music Hall, Washington 27/6/84
COMMENTS: Excellent FM radio broadcast. Red and yellow sleeve.

☐ "WE ARE HAVING A HEAVENLY TIME"
(P.F.M. Records Q-9022)

SIDE 1: Seven Chinese Brothers, Catapult, Radio Free Europe, Letter Never Sent, Kohoutek, So.

Roger, Bill, Mike & Pete Remember The Byrds

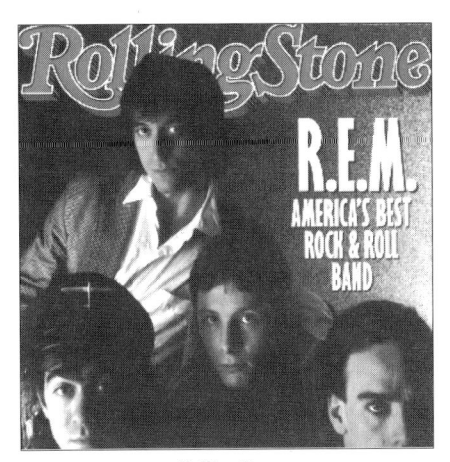

Rolling Stone

Smokin' In the Boys Room

So Much Younger Then

We're Blinking As Fast As We Can

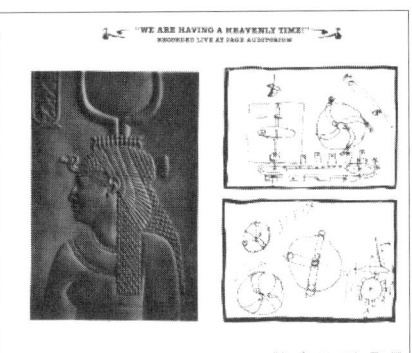

We Are Having A Heavenly Time

Central Rain (I'm Sorry).
SIDE 2: Driver 8, (Don't Go Back To) Rockville, 1,000,000 (not listed on cover), Hyena, Old Man Kensey, Second Guessing.

RECORDING DETAILS: Live at thePaige Auditorium, Durham, North Carolina 9/84
COMMENTS: Excellent soundboard recording but mastered too fast. Great black and white cover. Cover lists "Carnival Of Sorts" instead of "1,000,000".

☐ "WORKING"
(Auto Dight Records 1346)(Double LP)

SIDE 1: Finest Worksong, These Days, Welcome To The Occupation, Pilgrimage, Disturbance At The Heron House, Exhuming McCarthy, Don't Call On Me (Orange Crush).
SIDE 2: Feeling Gravity's Pull, King Of Birds, I Believe, Sitting Still, Ghost Riders In The Sky, Pretty Persuasion, Superman.
SIDE 3: Oddfellows Local 151, It's The End Of The World As We Know It (And I Feel Fine), Begin The Begin, 1,000,000,
 Wolves Lower.
SIDE 4: See No Evil, Pop Hit (Song) 89, Ghost Rider, Cuyahoga, Crazy.

RECORDING DETAILS: Live at the Universal Ampitheatre, Los Angeles, CA 15/11/87
COMMENTS: Very good audience recording. Issued in two different sleeves: one full-colour, one black white and red.

Working (black/white/red sleeve)   *Working (colour sleeve)*

BOOTLEG COMPILATIONS & OTHERS

Three REM tracks are included on the bootleg compilation **"THE 80'S DO THE 60'S: THE BEAT GOES ON"**(Double LP). An album called **"IT CRAWLED FROM THE SOUTH"** (after the name REM used for this low-key, all-covers gig) recorded at the Peppermint Lounge, New York is rumoured to exist as are discs entitled **"GREEN IN CONCERT - REM USA"**, **"I DON'T DO AUTOGRAPHS"**, **"R-4"**, **"RATIONAL EXTRAORDINARY MILKSHAKES"** and **"CAN'T GET THERE FROM HERE PART 3"** (of course some of these may duplicate material already available under different titles). Undoubtedly the flow of bootlegs will continue.

BOOTLEG 7" FLEXI-DISCS

All of the three bootleg flexi-discs that have emerged so far have been issued by the 'Borehole unofficial REM fan club'. Each comes in a folded, photocopied black & white paper sleeve.

☐ "CHESTNUT"
(MF01-X1)
SIDE 1: Tainted Obligations, The Ballad Of Cat Ballou
SIDE 2: Jazz Lips, Parade Of The Wooden Soldiers

RECORDING DETAILS: Side 1, track 1 by Community Trolls including Michael Stipe. Side 1 track 2 Michael Stipe & Peter Buck from US radio broadcast. Side 2 track 1, Drive-In Studio demo. Side 2 track 2, from REM Fan Club Xmas single 1989.
COMMENTS: Average recording quality, low volume. 1,000 copies pressed.

☐ "MIMED EP"
(MF02-X2)
SIDE 1: Benjamin Caroline Triangle, Rotary Thirteen.
SIDE 2: Wayward Wind, Half A World Away, These Days

RECORDING DETAILS: unknown
COMMENTS: Another disc presented by the unofficial 'Borehole' REM fan club. UK 1991

☐ "APPLAUD EP"
(MF03-X3)
SIDE 1: Low, Get Up.
SIDE 2: Kohoutek, Swan Swan H, Endgame.

RECORDING DETAILS: unknown
COMMENTS: third release from the 'Borehole' REM fan club, UK, 1991. Limited edition of 500 copies.

BOOTLEG COMPACT DISCS

When this discography was first published, as "A Few Chords & A Cloud Of Dust" in the autumn of 1990, there was just one REM bootleg CD available - "Standing Room Only" - as of this revised edition there are almost 40 titles available, surely a good measure of the band's improved standing in the rock'n'roll stratosphere over the past couple of years. Undoubtedly there would have been many more available had the band played live more often in the intervening period, too.

❑ "ACOUSTIC '87"
Nu Noize NUN 004
The One I Love, Welcome To The Occupation, Disturbance At The Heron House, Finest Worksong, Maps & Legends, Walk Don't Run/Baby Please Don't Go, A Million Miles Away, Trains, The One I Love, Spooky, Disturbance At The Heron House, Finest Worksong, Fever, So. Central rain (I'm Sorry), Leaving On A Jet Plane.

RECORDING DETAILS: Live at McCabe's Guitar Shop, Santa Monica, CA, USA 24/5/87.
COMMENTS: Amateurish audience recording - poor quality with crackling and a dulled sound. 'Million Miles Away' is a cover of the Plimsouls song featuring what sounds like original Plimsouls singer Peter Case on vocals.

❑ "ACOUSTIC TOUR '91"
Real Live RL CD 04
World Leader Pretend, Half A World Away, Radio Song, Love Is All Around, Losing My Religion, Fall On Me, It's The End Of The World As We Know It (And I Feel Fine), Belong, Low, Endgame, Swan Swan H, Spooky, Disturbance At The Heron House, Fretless, Dallas, Losing My Religion, World Leader Pretend.

RECORDING DETAILS: Tracks 1-5, 14 from East Sound Studio 1, Toronto, Ontario, Canada on 9th May 1991. Tracks 6-8, 16, 17 from "Mountain Stage" FM radio broadcast from Charleston, West Virginia, USA on 4th May 1991. Tracks 9-13, 15 from KCRW-FM "Snap" show, Los Angeles, 4th March 1991.
COMMENTS: Superb quality recordings throughout.

❑ "ANIMALS ATTRACTIONS"
Speedball Company SBC012
Half A World Away, Disturbance At The Heron House, Radio Song, Low, Perfect Circle, Fall On Me, Belong, Love Is All Around, It's The End Of The World As We Know It (And I Feel Fine), Losing my Religion, She Will Talk About The Weather (Pop Song '89).

RECORDING DETAILS: MTV's "Unplugged" live acoustic broadcast, New York, 1991.
COMMENTS: Excellent quality.

❑ "BLUE THE ACOUSTIC CONCERT"
Great Live Records GLR 9016
COMMENTS: same as "Animals Attractions" - some tracks incorrectly titled.

❑ "BOSTON 1984"
(Details unknown)
Moral Kiosk, Driver 8, Catapult, Hyena, Camera, Pilgrimage, Talk About The Passion, 7 Chinese

Acoustic '87

Accoustic Tour '91

Animals Attractions

Blue: The Acoustic Concert

Brothers, So. Central Rain, Pretty Persuasion, 9-9, Windout, Old man Kensey, Radio Free Europe, Little America, Burning Down, Plae Blue Eyes, 1,000,000, So You Want To Be A Rock'n'Roll Star, Carnival Of Sorts, Taking Out The Seeds (?)

RECORDING DETAILS: Live at the Orpheum, Boston, MA 19th July 1984
COMMENTS: Very good sound quality.

❏ "CARNIVAL OF SORTS"
Great Dane Records GDR CD 9020
Gardening At Night, 9-9, Ages Of You, Shaking Through, Laughing, Romance, Sitting Still, Pretty Persuasion, That Beat, Catapult, Radio Free Europe, Wolves Lower, Carnival Of Sorts (Boxcars), White Tornado, West Of The Fields, Stumble/Skank, There She Goes Again.

RECORDING DETAILS: Live at Merlins, Madison, WI, USA 24/4/82.
COMMENTS: Excellent, soundboard.

❏ "DISTURBANCES"
Heartsounds Records CA 784A
Femme Fatale, Radio Free Europe, Gardening At Night, 9-9, Wind Out, Letter Never Sent, Sitting Still, Little America, Second Guessing, (Don't Go Back To) Rockville, Driver 8, So. Central Rain (I'm Sorry), 7 Chinese Brothers, Pretty Persuasion, Second Guessing.

RECORDING DETAILS: Live at the Aragon Ballroom, Chicago, IL, 7th July 1984.
COMMENTS: Terrible sound quality.

❏ "THE DREAM - GREEN WORLD TOUR"
Red Phantom RPCD 1028
Exhuming McCarthy, Turn You Inside Out, Stand, Orange Crush, Feeling Gravity's Pull, King Of Birds, World Leader Pretend, Underneath The Bunker, Pretty Persuasion, Get Up, Auctioneer (Another Engine), It's The End Of The World As We Know It, Summertime, Swan Swan H, Finest Worksong, Begin The Begin, Perfect Circle, Dark Globe.

RECORDING DETAILS: Last 3 tracks live at Palatrussardi, Milan, Italy 15th June 1989, rest live at Pink Pop Festival, Landgraaf, Netherlands 15/5/89.
COMMENTS: Great packaging with fold-out colour insert. Excellent quality sound.

❏ "FROM THE BORDERLINE"
Red Phantom RPCD 2038/2039 (double CD)
Disc 1: Intro, World Leader Pretend, Half a World Away, Fretless, The One I Love, Hello In There, My Youngest Son, Jackson/Dallas, Disturbance at The Heron House, Belong, Low, Love Is All Around, You Are The Everything, Swan Swan H, Radio Song.
Disc 2: Perfect Circle, Endgame, Pop Song 89, Losing My Religion, Fall On Me (Parts 1 and 2), Tom's Diner, You Ain't Going Nowhere, Get Up, Moon River, Half A World Away, Swan Swan H, Belong, Driver 8, Low, Fretless, Losing My Religion.

RECORDING DETAILS: Live at the Borderline, London 15/3/89. Last 7 tracks from Shocking Club, Milan 22/3/91 - same as "Low" CD.
COMMENTS: Excellent audience recording. Beautiful slim-line double CD packaging and 2 full colour booklets. Whoever put this together got the date wrong and thinks "Bill Barry" is the bass player & Mike Mills plays drums. Otherwise it's wonderful.

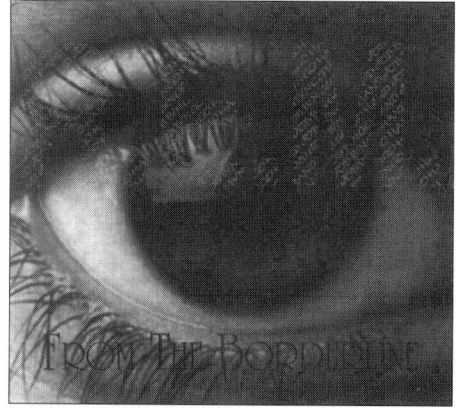

From The Borderline 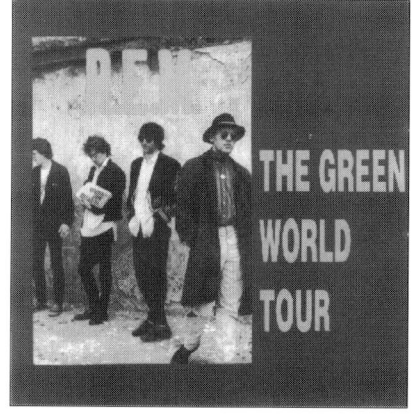   *The Green World Tour*

Boston 1984

Disturbances

The Dream

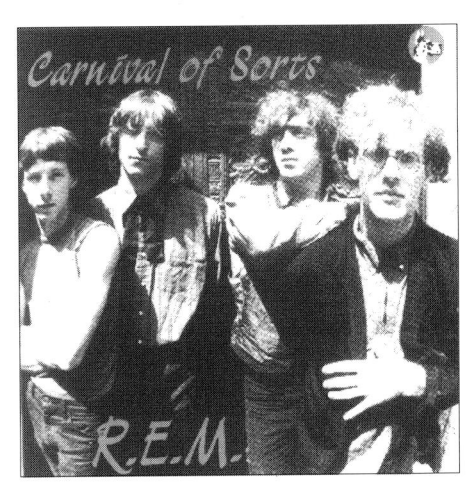

Carnival Of Sorts

❏ "THE GREEN WORLD TOUR"

RS Records CD18
Pop Song 89, These Days, Exhuming McCarthy, Turn You Inside Out, Orange Crush, Distrubance At The Heron House, Feeling Gravity's Pull, King Of Birds, Shaking Through, World Leader Pretend, Finest Worksong, Underneath The Bunker, Sitting Still, Get Up, Auctioneer (Another Engine), It's The End Of The World As We Know It (And I Feel Fine), Stand.

RECORDING DETAILS: Live at the Perugia Palasport, Italy, 17th June 1989.
COMMENTS: Good audience recording. Same set maybe available as "Rock Perugia 89" Insekt Records IS 011

❑ "HALF A WORLD AWAY" (PART ONE)
Mongoose Records MONG CD007A
World Leader Pretend, Half A World Away, Don't Talk To Me, Disturbance At The Heron House, Radio Song, Low, Love Is All Around, Academy Fight Song, Tusk, Dallas, Losing My Religion, Mary Tyler Moore Theme, Bandwagon, Endgame, Jackson, Swan Swan H, Spooky, Radio Ethiopia, Fall On Me, Deck The Halls, Parade Of The Wooden Soldiers, See No Evil, Good King Wenceslas, Academy Fight Song, Ghost Reindeer In The Sky, Summertime.

RECORDING DETAILS: Tracks 1 to 19 live in the studio, KCRW-FM, Los Angeles Deirdre O'Donahue Show 3/4/91. Track 20: from Warner Bros promo LP "Winter Warnerland". Tracks 21 to 26 from REM Fan Club Xmas singles 1988, 1989 and 1990.
COMMENTS: Excellent quality. Some slight wow & flutter at start.

❑ "HALF A WORLD AWAY" (PART TWO)
Mongoose Records MONG CD007B
Half A World Away, Disturbance At The Heron House, Radio Song, Low, Perfect Circle, Fall On Me, Untitled, Love Is All Around, It's The End Of The World, Losing My Religion, Pop Song '89, Endgame, Halfd A World Away, Radio Song, Love Is All Around, Losing My Rerligion (Rockline, Losing My Religion, Shiny Happy People.

RECORDING DETAILS: Tracks 1-13 MTV 'Unplugged' TV broadcast 24/4/91. Tracks 14-16 'Rockline' radio show 1/4/91. Tracks 17-18 'Saturday Night Live' TV Show 24/4/91)
COMMENTS: Excellent quality.

❑ "IN THE YEAR 2525"
Great Live Records GLR 9109
There She Goes Again, In The Year 2525, Eight Miles High (/Roadrunner), Have You Ever Seen The Rain, What's New Pussycat, Radar Love, Gloria, Rave On, Pale Blue Eyes, So You Wanna be a Rock'n'roll Star, Moon River, paint It Black, California Dreaming, Femme Fatale, Toys In The Attic, See No Evil, Hey Little Girl, The Lion Sleeps Tonight, Behind Closed Doors, Fall On Me, Smokin' In The Boys Room, Sweet Home Alabama.

RECORDING DETAILS: A collection of live cover versions recorded between 1981 and 1990.
COMMENTS: Quality varies between average and very good - overall it's very listenable. The compilers presumably are unaware that 'Fall On Me' is an original REM composition and not a cover of the Moby Grape song.

Half A World Away, Part One    *Half A World Away, Part Two*

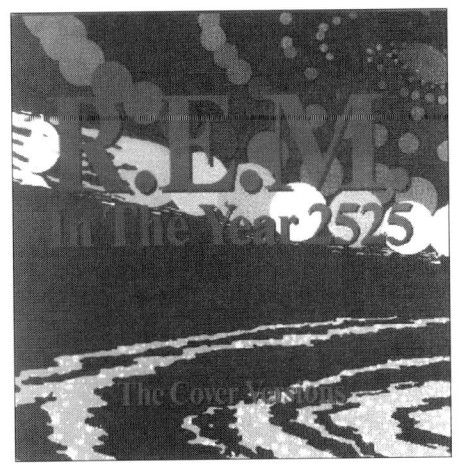

In The Year 2525    *It's The End Of The World*

❏ "IT'S THE END OF THE WORLD"
Kiss The Stone KTS 005
Pop Song '89, Exhuming McCarthy, Welcome To The Occupation, Disturbance At The Heron House, Turn You Inside Out, Orange Crush, Feeling Gravity's Pull, Swan Swan H, Begin The Begin, Pretty Persuasion, I Believe, King Of Birds, Crazy, Finest Worksong, You Are The Everything, Academy Fight Song, Stand, Perfect Circle, Get Up, It's The End Of The World As We Know It (And I Feel Fine).

RECORDING DETAILS: Live in Orlando, Florida, 30th April 1989, during the "Green World Tour". Previously broadcast on US radio.
COMMENTS: Excellent sound quality. 76.14 minutes.

❏ "LIVE COLLECTION"
Living Legend Records LLRCD153
Gardening At Night, RFE, White Tornado, West Of The Fields, There She Goes Again, Pop Song 89, Listen To Me, Turn You Inside Out, Orange Crush, Swan Swan H, Begin The Begin, Stand, Perfect cicle, Get Up, It's The End Of The World, Losing My Religon, Half A World Away, Radio Song, Love Is All Around.

RECORDING DETAILS: Tracks 1-5 Recorded live in Madison 1982; Tracks 6-15 Seattle 1989; Tracks 16-19 Live in New York 1991.
COMMENTS: Very good/excellent quality recordings.

❏ "LOVE AND SQUALOR"
Howdy Records CD 555 - 07
Pop Song '89, Exhuming McCarthy, Welcome To The Occupation, Disturbance At The Heron House, Orange Crush, Feeling Gravity's Pull, Begin The Begin, Pretty Persuasion, I Believe, Swan Swan H, Flowers Of Guatemala, Crazy, Finest Worksong, You Are The Everything, Academy Fight Song, Stand, Perfect Circle, Get Up, It's The End Of The World As We Know (And I Feel Fine).

RECORDING DETAILS: recorded live on the Green Tour '88 says the cover - but it's the Orlando, Florida set from 1989 again!
COMMENTS: Excellent quality.

☐ "LOW"
Templar TCD 28
Disturbance At The Heron House, Half A World Away, Swan Swan H, Belong, Driver 8, Low, Fretless, Love Is All Around, Losing My Religion, Fall On Me, Get Up.

RECORDING DETAILS: An REM gig a la Bingo Hand Job but without the assistance of Spanish Charlie (Peter Holsapple) who had returned to the USA, before an invited audience of journalists, media types and liggers at the Shocking Club, Milan, Italy, 22/3/91. The set was broadcast locally on "Videomusic" TV show and "Rock Cafe" radio.
COMMENTS: Very good quality.

☐ "MAPS AND LEGENDS"
MONG CD005
Hello Stranger, The One I Love, Welcome To The Occupation, Disturbance At The Heron House, Finest Worksong, Maps & Legends, Baby Please Don't Go, 1,000,000 Miles Away, Hello Stranger, Campfire Song, Stretch Out My Hand (second set): The One I Love, Spooky, Disturbance, Finest Worksong, Fever, S. Central Rain.
RECORDING DETAILS: Live at McCabe's Guitar Shop, Santa Monica, CA, USA 24th May 1987.
COMMENTS: Poor recording - lots of wow'n'flutter. Taken from the same gig as 'Acoustic '87' but with a slightly different track list - sounds like the CD was mastered from the same cassette too.

☐ "OLD MAN KINSEY"
Hallmark HM 004CD
Hyena, Talk About The Passion, West Of The Fields, Rockville, Auctioneer, So. Central Rain, Sitting Still, Old Man Kensey, Gardening At Night, 9-9, Windout, Driver 8, Pretty Persuasion, Radio Free Europe.

RECORDING DETAILS Nottingham, BBC broadcast.
COMMENTS: Excellent quality.

Live Collection   *Low*

Love And Squalor

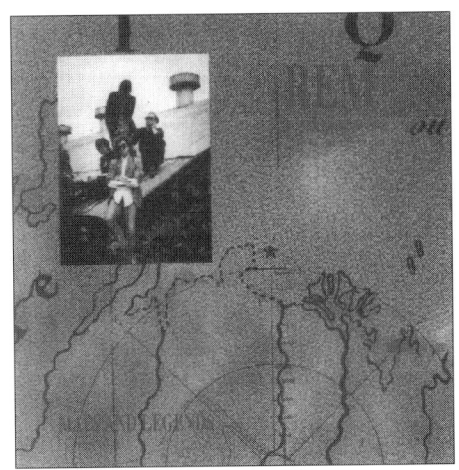

Maps And Legends

Old Man Kensey

Outtakes Of Time

☐ "OUTTAKES OF TIME"
no label R01
Radio Song, Belong (instrumental), Texarkana, It's A Free World Baby, Here I Am Again, Instrumental #1, Losing My religion, Instrumental #2, Shiny Happy People, Me In Honey, Endgame, Half A World Away, Sugar Cane, Radio Song, Near Wild Heaven, Fretless (instrumental), Low, 42nd Street Song, Country Feedback.

RECORDING DETAILS: "Out of Time" demos/outtakes
COMMENTS: Very good quality. A similar, but not identical set to "Slightly Out Of Time" listed later on in this section.

PAGE 91

☐ "PERFECT CIRCLE"
Pluto Records PLr CD 9136
Pop Song 89, Exhuming McCarthy Welcome To The Occupation, Disturbance At The Heron House, Turn You Inside Out, Orange Crush, Feeling Gravity's Pull, Swan Swan H, Begin The Begin, Pretty Persuasion, I Believe, King Of Birds, Crazy, Finest Worksong, You Are The Everything, Academy Fight Song, Stand, Perfect Circle, Get Up, It's The End Of The World As We Know It (And I Feel Fine).

RECORDING DETAILS: No details of origin on the sleeve, but this was taken from thebroadcast of theOrlando, Florida gig of 30th April 1989.
COMMENTS: Excellent quality

☐ "POETS OF THE WHEAT"
Beech Marten Records BM 049/2 (Double CD)
Disc 1: Don't Talk To Me, Me In Honey, Half A World Away, Radio Song, Losing My Religion, It's Written in The Wind (Love Is All Around), Pop Song '89, Exhuming McCarthy, Listen (To Me), Disturbance At The Heron House, Turn You Inside Out, Orange Crush, Feeling Gravity's Pull, Swan Swan H.
Disc 2: Begin The Begin, Pretty Persuasion, I Believe, King Of Birds, Crazy, Finest Worksong, You Are The Everything, Your Academy (Academy Fight Song), Stand, Perfect Circle, Get Up, It's The End Of The World As We Know It (And I Feel Fine).

RECORDING DETAILS: Disc 1: Tracks 1 - 6: from BBC TV "Late Night Line Up" broadcast. Tracks 7-14 and disc 2: tracks 1 - 12 cover says 'Recorded live in Seattle '89' - however they are all recorded at Orlando, Florida, 30th April 1989.
COMMENTS: All 20 Orlando tracks are available on other CDs ("It's The End Of The World"/"Love And Squalor"/"Perfect Circle") in similarly excellent quality.

☐ "PHILADELPHIA 1984"
On The Road GZCD 1010
Radio Free Europe, Hyena, Letter Never Sent, Camera, Gardening At Night, 9-9, Windout, (Don't Go Back To) Rockville, So. Central Rain, Little America, Second Guessing, Talk About The Passion, Wolves Lower, Moon River, Ghost Riders In The Sky, There She Goes Again, We Walk.

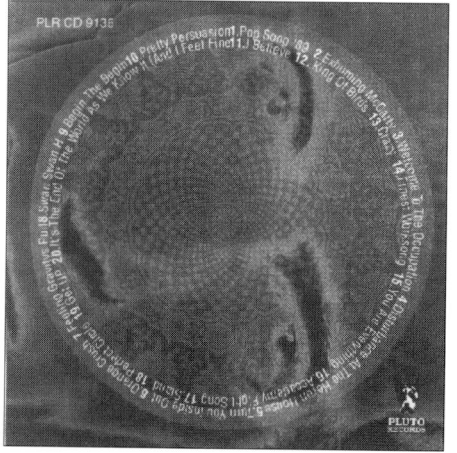

Perfect Circle

Philadelphia 1984

Poets Of The Wheat

Radio Song

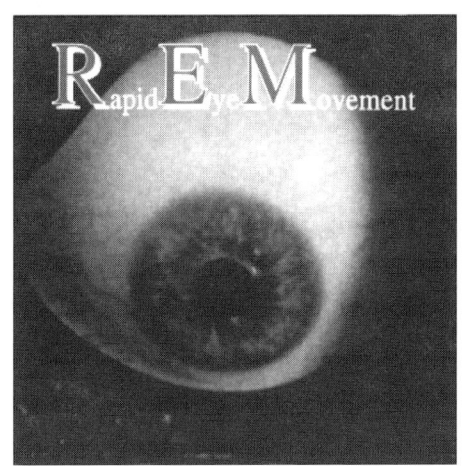

Rapid Eye Movement

Rapid Eye Movement On Tour

RECORDING DETAILS: Live at the Tower Theatre, Philadelphia, USA 17/10/84.
COMMENTS: Very good quality. Also issued as "Rapid Eye Movement: On Tour" (same label/cat. no) in a different, but still boring, sleeve. Same track list.

❏ "RADIO SONG"
On Stage Records OS CD 3
Radio Song, Losing My Religion, Fretless, Me In Honey, Half A World Away, Love Is All Around, Swan Swan H, Begin The Begin, Pop Song 89, Turn You Inside Out, You Are The Everything, Perfect Circle.

RECORDING DETAILS: Sleeve says "Recorded live during the 80's" but these are 1991 recordings.
COMMENTS: Excellent quality sound.

❑ "RAPID EYE MOVEMENT"
Turtle Records TR-08
Finest Worksong, These Days, Lightning Hopkins, Welcome To The Occupatin, Driver 8, Feeling Gravity's Pull, I Believe, The One I Love, Exhuming McCarthy, Wolves - Lower, Fall On Me, Superman, Just A Touch, Oddfellows local 151, Little America, Hyena, Driver 8, Old Man Kensey, Pretty Persuasion, 1,000,000.
RECORDING DETAILS: Tracks 1 to 15 live at the Muziekcentrum, Utrecht, Netherlands 14/9/87 (date incorrectly shown on cover as 19/9/87). All of these tracks - plus more - appear on the "Standing Room Only" CD but in inferior sound quality. Tracks 16 to 20 live in Olso, Norway 6/10/85.
COMMENTS: Very good quality. Excellent colour fold-out digi-pak.

❑ "RAPID EYE MOVEMENT: ON TOUR"
On The Road GZCD 1010
COMMENTS: same as "Philadelphia 1984". Different sleeve, but still boring.

❑ "ROCK'N'ROLL STARS"
Howdy Records CD 555-19
Moral Kiosk, Hyena, Camera, Pilgrimage, Talk About The Passion, 7 Chinese Brothers, So. Central Rain (i'm Sorry), Pretty Persuasion, Gardening At Night, 9-9, Wind Out, Old Man Kinsey, Radio Free Europe, Little America, Burning Down, Pale Blue Eyes, 1,000,000, So You Wanna Be A Rock'n'Roll Star, Carnival of Sorts (Boxcars), Skank.

RECORDING DETAILS: Live in Seattle, Washington, 27th June 1984
COMMENTS: Good colour sleeve. Excellent quality.

❑ "SEATTLE 1989 (IT'S THE END OF THE WORLD)
On The Road RSCD 1124 (2 CD set)
DISC 1: Pop Song 89, Exhuming McCarthy, Welcome To The Occupation, Disturbance At The Heron House, Turn You Inside Out, Orange Crush, Feeling Gravity's Pull, Swan Swan H, Begin The Begin, Pretty Persuasion, I Believe, King Of Birds, Crazy, Finest Worksong, You Are The Everything, Academy Fight Song, Stand, Perfect Circle, Get Up, It's The End Of The Wor;ld As We Know It (And I Feel Fine).
DISC 2: Losing My Religion, Half A World Away, Radio Song, Love Is All Around

RECORDING DETAILS: Disc 1 is not from Seattle but is the Orlando, Florida 1989 show again. The second disc, entitled "REM Acoustic 1991" comes in a cardboard slipcase shrink-wrapped to the main CD - all 4 tracks are from the BBC Radio 1 session of 13th March 1991.
COMMENTS: Excellent quality.

❑ "SLIGHTLY OUT OF TIME"
(no name on label) 92-R-14-07
Radio Song, Belong (instrumental version), Texarkana, Losing My Religion, Instrumental (Speed Metal), Shiny Happy People, Me In Honey, Half A World Away, Losing My Religon (version), Radio Song (acoustic version),, Near Wild Heaven, Instrumental (Fretless), Low, Country Feedback, Ghost Riders (Ghost Reindeer In The Sky), Gave Too Much Away (It's A Free World Baby), Here I Am Again, New Song, Endgame.

RECORDING DETAILS: Studio demos/outtakes recorded for the "Out Of Time" album at John Keane Studios, Athens, GA, early-mid 1990.
COMMENTS: Very good quality. Cheekily uses the same basic sleeve design as the official "Out Of Time" album. A similar, but not identical set to "Outtakes of Time" listed earlier.

Rock'n'Roll Stars 　　　　　　　　　*Seattle 1984*

Bonus disc included with Seattle 1984 　　　　　　　　　*Slightly Out Of Time*

☐ "SONGS FOR A GREEN WORLD"
Flashback Records FB150
COMMENTS: Oh dear, it's that Orlando, Florida show from 1989 again!

☐ "STAB IT AND STEER IT"
Adobe Music CD RAIN 1
That Beat, Pretty Persuasion, All The Right Friends, Tighten Up, There She Goes Again, Moon River, Theme From Two Steps Onward, When I Was Young, Bad Day, The Lion Sleeps Tonight, Skank, Walters Theme, Cushy Tush, Gardening At Night (acoustic version), Mystery To Me, Gardening At Night (acoustic version 2), Tainted Obligation.

RECORDING DETAILS: Tracks 1-6, 14-16 Reflection Studio demos, Charlotte, North Carolina, January 1983. Track 7 live at the Stock Pavillion, Madisoion, WI, 10 May 1985. 8 live at Brown University,

Povidence, RI, 27th April 1985. 9 Studio demo 1986. 10-13 Rhythmic Studios, San Francisco, 9th November 1983. 17 Community Trolls recording featuring Michael Stipe.
COMMENTS: Good quality, but much hiss evident throughout. Unimaginative sleeve design.

❏ "STANDING ROOM ONLY"
Swingin' Pigs Records - no catalogue number

Finest Worksong, These Days, Lightnin' Hopkins, Welcome To The Occupation, Driver 8, Feeling Gravity's Pull, I Believe, The One I Love, Exhuming McCarthy, Wolves Lower, Fall One Me, Superman, Just A Touch, Oddfellows Local 151, Strange, Disturbance At The Heron House, Funtime, Moral Kiosk, Life And How To Live It.

RECORDING DETAILS: Recorded live at the Muziekcentrum, Utrecht, Netherlands 14/9/87.
COMMENTS: Good soundboard quality recording, although bass heavy and with variable sound levels. Most, but not all of these tracks are available in better quality on the "Rapid Eye Movement" CD - see earlier entry."Standing Room Only" was the first REM bootleg CD title to appear, around the summer of 1990. It didn't remain alone for long though....

❏ "STREET OF MILLIONAIRES"
Raid Masters CD 910709

Laughing, Pilgrimage, There She Goes Again, Seven Chinese Brothers, Talk About The Passion, Sitting Still, Harbor Coat, Catapult, Gardening At Night, 9-9, Just A Touch, West Of The Fields, Radio Free Europe, We Walk, 1,000,000.

RECORDING DETAILS: cover says "Live in San Francisco 1983" but the recording is in fact from a gig at Larry's Hideaway, Toronto, Canada in 1983.
COMMENTS: Very good quality, sounds a trifle 'thin'.

❏ "THAT BEAT IN TIME"
O.M.K. Records OMKCD 001

Hey! Hey! Nadine, Burning Down, Dangerous Times, There She Goes Again, Rockville, Body Count, Just A Touch, Sitting Still, Permanent Vacation, Get On Their Way, Shaking Through, Romance,

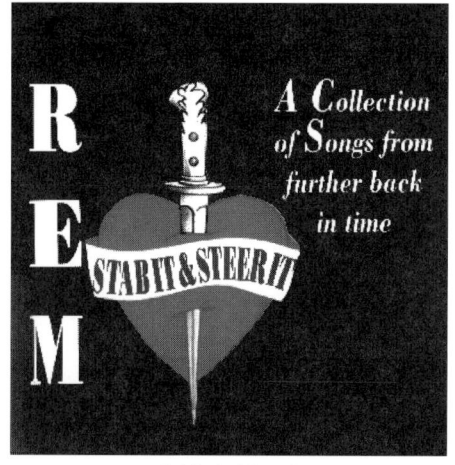

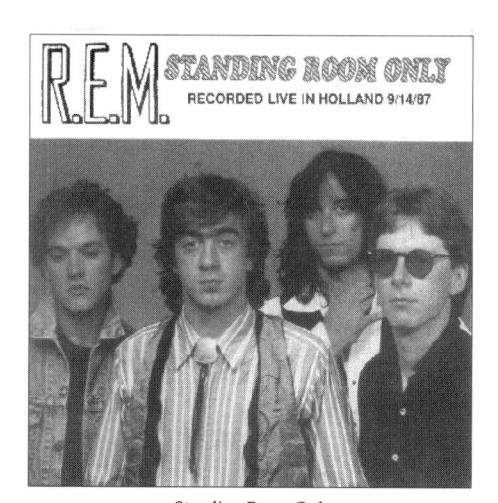

Stab It And Steer It   *Standing Room Only*

Street Of Millionaires   *That Beat In Time*

Laughing, Pretty Persuasion, That Beat, Stumble, Radio Free Europe, Carnival Of Sorts (Boxcars), Skank, Windout, Gardening At Night, White Tornado.

RECORDING DETAILS: Live at Tyrone's, Athens, GA, USA, 12th may 1981.
COMMENTS: Superb, soundboard recording with lots of early songs. Two slightly different cover designs have been noted - these are best differenciated by looking at the rear sleeve. On the original rear sleeve the text is superimposed on a picture of Stipe's head, while the later version has a plain black background under the text.

❑ "TIME OF OUTTAKES"
(no label) CD-9201
Half A World Away, Night Swim, Fretless, instrunental, Texarkana, It's A Free World Baby, Low, Endgame, Radio Song (soft), Country Feedback, Losing My Religion, Speed Metal, Kerouac No.4, Near Wild Heaven, Shiny Happy People, Belong, Radio Song (hard), Me In Honey.

RECORDING DETAILS: Studio recordings from Bearsville Studios, NY, winter 1990. 'Out Of Time' outtakes/demos.
COMMENTS: Excellent quality - better than both the similarly sourced "Slightly Out Of Time" and "Outtakes Of Time" CDs. No wonder the originators of this disc are without a label - these anonymous and cheeky devils have used graphics taken exclusively from the 'Few Chords' book for their cover design!!

❑ "20TH CENTURY BOYS VOL.1"
(no name on label) REM-92-SC
I Got You Babe, Here We Are (?), Harborcoat, Pretty Persuasion, Pills, Millions Like Us, Camera, Talk About The Passion, Little America, Party Girl, Letter Never Sent, Just A Touch, Secret Agent Man, Hootenany, Route 66, Wind Out, Don't Know, 6 Stock Answers To 74,000 Questions, My Roof Your Roof, Pale Blue Eyes, Tainted Obligations.

RECORDING DETAILS: Cover says recorded live at the 'Wind-Up' Club, Athens, GA, USA, 1983 (actually it's from the Mad Hatter in the autumn of '83)
COMMENTS: Excellent soundboard recording. Excellent colour packaging.

☐ **"20TH CENTURY BOYS VOL.2"**
(no name on label) REM-92-SC
Rave On, 20th Century Boy, 7 Chinese Brothers, Crazy, Remember Me, (Don't Go Back To) Rockville, Carnival Of Sorts (Boxcars), Just A Touch, Nervous Breakdown, A Girl Like You, Dangerous Times, There She Goes Again, This And That, Party Girl, (Don't Go Back To) Rockville, Body Count, Hippy Hippy Shake, Action, Narrator (Jacques Cousteau), Small Town Girl, Gardening At Night, Sheherazade, Lisa Said, It's A Mystery, Get Stoned, Permanent Vacation.

RECORDING DETAILS: Tracks 1-7 cover says live at the 'Wind-Up' Club, Athens, GA, USA, 1983 (actually it's the Mad Hatter, in the Autumn of '83). Tracks 8-26 live at Tyrones, Athens, GA, USA, spring 1980 - one of the very first REM gigs!
COMMENTS: Companion volume to above. Excellent soundboard recordings (both gigs) and excellent colour packaging.

Time Of Outtakes

20th Century Boys, Vol.1

20th Century Boys, Vol.2

LIVE TAPES, GIGS & RECORDING SESSIONS

LIVE TAPES, GIGS & RECORDING SESSIONS

A listing of live tapes can never hope to be absolutely complete. With the advent of the small portable recording Walkman-type cassette recorders during the 1980's, it is entirely possible that almost every gig REM has played has been recorded by at least one person in the audience - some people will trade these tapes so that they pass into general circulation, others do not. The quality of the original tapes and copies of them can, of course vary infinitely, thus what follows is a comprehensive listing of all known R.E.M. gigs between 1980 and 1992; where it is known that a tape of a particular gig is in circulation we have indicated thus ✦. As several different tapes of variable recording quality may originate from the same gig, have not given a quality rating, although we have indicated where tapes are of soundboard, radio or TV broadcast origin and so potentially of superior fidelity. In view of the large number of tapes in circulation, it is not feasable to give track listings for the majority of tapes, although we have included comments on representative, or particularly notable performances.

1980

Most of the gigs in the band's first year of existence were within the boundaries of their home state of Georgia - though they did stray as far afield as North Carolina on occasion! No recordings were issued until the following year - although R.E.M. did record some rough, live demos at one of their favourite local haunts - until it burned down - Tyrone's.

St. Mary's Episcopal Church, Athens, GA, USA 5/4/80
   (Their first ever gig, with Turtle Bay & Side Effects)
Koffee Club, Athens, GA, USA 19/4/80
Tyrone's, Athens, GA, USA 5/5/80
   (supporting The Brains)
Tyrone's, Athens, GA, USA 12/5/80
Memorial Hall, UGA Campus, Athens, GA, USA 15/5/80
   (supporting The Brains)
The Madhatter, Athens, GA, USA 30/6/80
The Station, Carrboro, NC, USA 18-19/7/80
   (First gig outside Georgia)
The Pier, Raleigh, NC, USA 21/7/80
Tyrone's, Athens, GA, USA 22/9/80
Tyrone's, Athens, GA, USA 23/9/80
Tyrone's, Athens, GA, USA (soundboard) .... 4/10/80 ✦
   (SET: Nervous Breakdown, A Girl Like You, Dangerous Times,
   There She Goes Again, I Can Only Give You Everything, All The

Right Friends, (Don't Go Back To) Rockville, Body Count, Hippy
Hippy Shake, Action, Narrator, She's Such A Pretty Girl,
Gardening At Night, Scherezade, Lisa Says, Mystery To Me,
Gloria, White Tornado).
Fox Theatre, Atlanta, GA, USA 6/12/80
  (supported The Police)
Tyrone's, Athens, GA, USA .... late 1980   ◆
  (Demo session. Tracks: Dangerous Times (2.12), All The Right Friends (3.50),
  A Different Girl (3.39), Narrator (2.48), Just A Touch (2.11),
  Baby I (2.19), Mystery To Me (2.00), Permanent Vacation (2.01))
Other 1980 gigs included 688 Club, Atlanta, GA; The Warehouse, Atlanta, GA and Fridays, Greensboro, NC.

1981

This year saw the band really starting to get into it's stride. In addition to the live appearances, they also record demos and tracks for their debut single "Radio Free Europe" and, later, mini-LP "Chronic Town" (completed and released the following year). For a period of about two months early in the year, Bill Berry also found the time to play gigs with the band Love Tractor.

Tyrone's, Athens, GA, USA (soundboard) ....10/1/81   ◆
Tyrone's, Athens, GA, USA 24/1/81
Bombay Studio, Smyra, GA, USA 8/2/81
  (Demo session: unreleased versions of 'Sitting Stll', 'Gardening At Night',
  'Radio Free Europe', 'Shaking Through', 'Mystery To Me', '(Don't Go Back To)
  Rockville', 'Narrator' and 'White Tornado'. Produced by Joe Perry)
Drive-In Studio, Winston-Salem, NC, USA ....5/3/81   ◆
  (demo: Jazz Lips)
Cantrell's, Nashville, TN, USA 27/3/81
The Milestone, Charlotte, NC, USA 28/3/81
Fridays, Greensboro, NC, USA 31/3/81
New York New York, Augusta, GA, USA 2/4/81
Vanderbilt, Nashville, TN, USA 3/4/81
The Station, Carrboro, USA 4/4/81
The Pier, Raleigh, NC, USA 6/4/81
Drive-In Studio, Winston Salem, NC, USA ....15/4/81   ◆
  (Hibtone single: Radio Free Europe/Sitting Still, and White Tornado.
  Producer Mitch Easter also mixed his own bizarre version of "Radio
  Free Europe (Radio dub)")
Tyrone's, Athens, GA, USA 12/5/81
  ('That Beat In Time' bootleg CD taken from this show)
Drive-In Studio, Winston-Salem, NC, USA 25/5/81
  (REM return to remix 'Radio Free Europe' for Hib-Tone 7")
40 Watt Club, Athens, GA, USA 5/81
  (One-off gig by Gaggle O'Sound - aka Michael Stipe!)
The Ritz, New York City, NY, USA 16-17/6/81

(support to Gang Of Four)
Pilgrim Theatre, New York City, NY, USA 16/9/81
Drive-In Studio, Winston-Salem, NC, USA .... 2-4 & 7/10/81 ✦
("Chronic Town" 12" tracks & outtakes: 1,000,000 (3 versions:
3.04/2.57/3.12), Ages Of You (3.17), Gardening At Night (3 versions:
4.33/3.21/3.33), Carnival Of Sorts (Boxcars) (4 versions:
3.51/3.38/3.36/3.55, Stumble, Shaking Through (2 versions: 3.47/4.01),
White Tornado (1.43), Wolves, Lower (3 versions: 4.08/4.04/4.02)).
Friday's, Greensboro, NC, USA 10/81
Mudd Club, New York, USA 10/81
Viceroy Park, Charlotte, NC, USA .... 7/11/81 ✦
Merlyn's, Madison, WI, USA .... 17/11/81 ✦
First Avenue, Minneapolis, MN, USA (soundboard) .... 25/11/81 ✦
(SET: Easy Come Easy Go, Sitting Still, Mystery To Me, Carnival
Of Sorts (Boxcars), Ages Of You, There She Goes Again, Pretty
Persuasion, Stumble, Permanent Vacation, Gardening At Night,
9-9, Windout, That Beat, Wolves Lower, White Tornado,
Radio Free Europe, Skank).
Tyrone's, Athens, GA, USA (soundboard) .... 5/12/81 ✦

1982

R.E.M. signed their first major recording contract, with IRS, after the one-off single on Hib-Tone the previous year. The mini-LP "Chronic Town" was the first IRS release. On the live front the band relentlessly pursued the audience that they knew was out there somewhere...

Drive-In Studio, Winston-Salem, NC, USA 27-28/1/82
  (Additional songs recorded for the aborted Dasht Hopes project)
Maxwells, Hoboken, NJ, USA 30/1/82
  (with The Neats)
RCA Studio C, New York City, NY, USA .... 1-2/2/82 ✦
Danceteria, New York City, NY, USA 3-4/2/82
RCA Studio C, New York City, NY, USA 8/2/82
  (7 demos recorded for RCA label during this and two day session a week earlier)
Beat Exchange, New Orleans, LA, USA 12/3/82
Merlyns, Madison, WI, USA (soundboard) .... 24/4/82 ✦
First Avenue, Minneapolis, MN, USA (soundboard) .... 26/4/82 ✦
Detroit, MI, USA 4/82
Atlanta Arts Festival, Piedmont Park, Atlanta, GA, USA .... 14/5/82 ✦
  (FM radio broadcast)
Drive-In Studio, NC, USA .... 31/5/82 ✦
  (Slow version of "Wolves, Lower" only)
1+1 Club, Athens, GA, USA .... 6/82 ✦

Legion Field, Athens, GA, USA 6/82
Toads Place, New Haven, CT, USA .... 10/6/82 ◆
    (SET: Gardening At Night, 9-9, Pilgrimage, Wolves-Lower, Easy Come
    Easy Go, Sitting Still, 1,000,000, Pretty Persuasion, Moral Kiosk, Catapult,
    West Of The Fields, Radio Free Europe, Perfect Circle, White Tornado,
    Ages Of You, We Walk, Carnival Of Sorts (Boxcars), Skank.)
Stand Cabaret, Marietta, GA, USA .... 2/7/82 ◆
The Agora Club, Miami, FL, USA 12/7/82
Music Machine, Los Angeles, CA, USA 19/8/82
Old Waldorf, San Francisco, CA, USA (FM radio broadcast)) .... 24/8/82 ◆
Club Lingerie, Los Angeles, CA, USA 8/82
    (Video for 'Wolves-Lower' shot at this gig)
KQAK-FM radio, CA, USA 8/82
    (interview)
First Avenue, Minneapolis, MN, USA 22/9/82
Huff Gym, Champaign, Ill, USA (soundboard) .... 24/9/82 ◆
University Of Illinois, Carbondale, PA, USA 9/82
Toad's Place, New Haven, CT, USA .... 6/10/82 ◆
Marble Bar, Baltimore, MD, USA 9/10/82
    (REM supported by Peter Holsapple they join him onstage to
    play the dB's "Neverland", later he joins them to play "Gardening
    At Night". REM set also includes versions of "Wipeout" and the
    Cramps' "Drug Train").
The Pier, Raleigh, NC, USA 10/10/82
Maxwells, Hoboken, NJ, USA 28/10/82
Georgia Technical College, Atlanta, GA, USA 31/10/82
Legion Field, Athens, GA, USA 10/82
Atlanta Agora, Atlanta, GA, USA 10/82
The Bayou, Baton Rouge, LA, USA 5/11/82
Tupelo's Tavern, New Orleans, LA, USA .... 6/11/82 ◆
WUTL radio station, Tulane University, New Orleans, LA, USA .... 6/11/82 ◆
    (FM radio interview)
City Gardens, Trenton, NJ, USA .... 16/11/82 ◆
    ('B-Sharp Concert Series' FM broadcast taken from above)
WUTK radio station, University of Tennessee, Knoxville, TN, USA .... 19/11/82 ◆
    (FM radio interview)
Hobo's, Knoxville, TN, USA 19/11/82
Nashville, TN, USA 20/11/82
Antenna Club, Memphis, TN, USA 21/11/82
Illinois, USA 22/11/82
Nassau Coliseum, Uniondale, NY, USA 24/11/82
    (Supporting Squeeze and The Beat)
Peppermint Lounge, New York, USA .... 25/11/82 ◆
    (SET: Gardening At Night, 9-9, Moral Kiosk, Pilgrimage, Shaking Through,
    7 Chinese Brothers, Wolves - Lower, Easy Come Easy Go, Sitting Still,
    Catapult, 1,000,000, West Of The Fields, Radio Free Europe, White Tornado,
    instrumental, We Walk, Judy, Neverland, Carnival Of Sorts (Boxcars).)
Agora Club, Miami, FL, USA 7/12/82
(unknown studio), Atlanta, GA, USA 12/82
    (Recorded demo of 'Catapult')

1983

The first album, "Murmur" was released this year. The band spent much of the year touring the USA, but, in November, played their first overseas gigs, in Europe. On their return to the USA, just before Christmas, work began on the "Reckoning" LP.

Reflection Studios, Charlotte, NC, USA .... 1/83 ◆
   ("Murmur" LP and outtakes including: Ages Of You (3.39), Burning Down (3.59) - both later included on an IRS double-pack single - There She Goes Again (issued as B-side of IRS "Radio Free Europe" single, That Beat (3.27), Pretty Pursuasion (3.52), All The Right Friends (3.43), Tighten Up (later issued on a flexi with "Bucketfull Of Brains" magazine), Moon River (1.46) and White Tornado)).
9.30 Club, Washington, DC, USA 12/3/83
9.30 Club, Washington, DC, USA (soundboard) .... 18/3/83 ◆
   (Mitch Easter guests)
Page Auditorium, Duke University, Durham, NC, USA 26/3/83
Memorial Hall, University Of North Carolina, Chapel Hill, NC, USA 27/3/83
University Of Miami, Coral Gables, FL, USA 31/3/83
Palestra University, Rochester, NY, USA .... 18/4/83 ◆
   (Tracks appear on "LIVE" bootleg LP)
Spize, New York City, NY, USA 26/4/83
The Ritz, New York City, NY, USA 30/4/83
The Pier, Raleigh, NC, USA .... 3/5/83 ◆
PB Scott's Music Hall, Blowing Rock, NC, USA 4/5/83
Navy Island, St. Paul, MN, USA 21/5/83
Headliners, Madison, WI, USA 23/5/83
Red Rocks Amphiteatre, Morrison, CO, USA 1/6/83
Old Waldorf, San Francisco, CA, USA .... 14/6/83 ◆
Keystone, Berkeley, CA, USA .... 20/6/83 ◆
   (SET: Moral Kiosk, Catapult, Laughing, Pilgrimage, 7 Chinese Brothers, Talk About The Passion, Wolves - Lower, Easy Come Easy Go, Sitting Still, Pretty Persuasion, Gardening At Night, 9-9, West Of The Fields, Radio Free Europe, Shaking Through, 1,000,000, Carnival Of Sorts (Boxcars))
The Blue Note, Columbia, SC, USA 28/6/83
St. Andrews Hall, Detroit, MI, USA 8/7/83
Larry's Hideaway, Toronto, Canada (soundboard) .... 9/7/83 ◆
   (aslo 60 minute FM broadcast of part of the above)
Paradise Theatre, Boston, MA, USA .... 13/7/83 ◆
   (FM radio broadcast of gig on WBCN-FM)
WCBN FM Radio, Boston, MA, USA .... 13/7/83 ◆
   (Interview with Peter Buck)
Toad's Place, New Haven, CT, USA .... 17/7/83 ◆
Ripley's Music Hall, Philadelphia, PA, USA (soundboard) .... 20/7/83 ◆
   (supported by The Replacements)
'Live At Five' TV Show, NBC TV, USA .... 17/8/83 ◆
   (Interview with Peter Buck & Mike Mills)
Shea Stadium, Queens, NY, USA 18/8/83
   (REM support the Police and Joan Jett & The Blackhearts - also next 2 gigs. Stipe introduces the band as "The Beatles" and they play a 5-song, 20 minute set. Their biggest gig to date)

Mike Mills. Photo by Derek Pringle.

JFK Stadium, Philadelphia, PA, USA	20/8/83 ♦
Capitol Centre, Largo, MD, USA	21/8/83
MTV, USA	21/8/83 ♦

(TV interview with Peter Buck & Mike Mills)

Legion Field, Athens, GA, USA	3/10/83
'Late Night With David Letterman' TV Show, NBC TV, NYC, NY, USA	6/10/83 ♦
Irwin Auditorium, Philadelphia, PA, USA	8/10/83
The Good Knight Pub, Piscathaway, NJ, USA	9/10/83 ♦

(SET: Moral Kiosk, Catapult, Letter Never Sent, Shaking Through, Pilgrimage, Seven Chinese Brothers, Talk About The Passion, So. Central Rain, Harborcoat, Sitting Still, Just a Touch, Pretty Persuasion, West Of The Fields, Second Guessing, Gardening At Night, 9-9, Windout, Radio Free Europe, Camera, We Walk, Little America, 1,000,000, Wolves Lower, 20th Century Boy, Pills, Carnival Of Sorts (Boxcars)).

NY, USA	12/10/83
Providence, Rhode Island, USA	13/10/83
Orono, ME, USA	14/10/83
Colby College, Waterville, ME, USA	15/10/83
Drumlins, Syracuse, NY, USA	17/10/83 ♦
Queens College, NYC, USA	21/10/83 ♦
Peppermint Lounge, New York City, NY, USA (soundboard)	31/10/83 ♦

(REM billed as It Crawled from The South, supporting The Cramps. They play an all covers set: 20th Century Boy, I Can't Control Myself, Crazy, Pale Blue Eyes, So You Want To Be A Rock'n'Roll Star, Femme Fatale, Secret Agent Man, Burning Hell, Pills, DOA, I Can Only Give You Everything).

'Livewire' TV Show, Nickleodeon TV, New York, USA	10/83 ♦
Rhythmic Studios, San Francisco, CA, USA	9/11/83 ♦

(24 demos recorded in one day! That Beat (2.46), Walter's Theme (1.21), Walters Barbeque Ad (.40), Cushy Tush Ad (.48), Burning Down (4.03), All The Right Friends (3.05), Windout (1.47), Femme Fatale (2.38), Burning Hell (3.23), The Lion Sleeps Tonight (2.21), Skank (4.41), All The Right Friends (3.31), So. Central Rain (I'm Sorry) (3.02), Letter Never Sent (2.54), Little America (2.45), Camera (5.04), Second Guessing (2.41), Second Guessing (2.41), Harborcoat (3.28), 7 Chinese Brothers (4.09), Just A Touch (2.27), Pretty Persuasion (3.40), Pale Blue Eyes (2.40), Time After Time (3.00))

Kabuki Theatre, San Francisco, CA, USA	10/11/83 ♦

(Set includes a version of the Velvet Underground's "Sweet Jane" with members of the Gang Of Four)

Beverly Theatre, Los Angeles, CA, USA	11/11/83
Montezuma Hall, SDSU Campus, San Diego, CA, USA	12/11/83
The Tube, TV Show, Newcastle, UK	18/11/83 ♦
Dingwalls, Camden, London, UK	19/11/83
The Marquee, London, UK	22/11/83 ♦
The Paradiso, Amsterdam, Netherlands	23/11/83
Les Bains Douches, Paris, France (FM radio broadcast)	24/11/83 ♦
Exo-7, Rouen, France	25/11/83 ♦
St. Petersburg, FL, USA	28/11/83
Reflection Sound Studios, Charlotte, NC, USA	8-10 & 12-15/12/83

(Beginning of sessions for "Reckoning" LP - see 1984 below also)

1984

This was a very busy year for the band with extensive gigging in the USA, their first dates in Japan and two visits to Europe. Additionally, R.E.M. finished recording the "Reckoning" album and Buck, Berry and Mills even found the time to play a couple of gigs as the Hindu Love Gods with either Bryan Cook or Warren Zevon taking the lead vocal!

Reflection Sound Studios, Charlotte, NC, USA .... 10-16/1/84 ◆
("Reckoning" and outtakes including Ages Of You (3.24), Burning Down (3.51) - both later included on "Dead Letter Office"-, Windout (1.47), Windout (1.46), White Tornado (1.40, later issued by IRS), Gardening At Night (acoustic, 2 versions: 3.30 & 4.21), Just A Touch (2.22), Mystery To Me (1.57), Voice Of Harold (issued as B-side of "So. Central Rain" 12"), Pale Blue Eyes (issued as B-side of "So. Central Rain" 12"), Femme Fatale (issued as "The Bob" flexi & later by IRS), King Of The Road (issued as B-side of "So. Central Rain" 7"), Walter's Theme (1.22), Burning Hell (instrumental version)
40 Watt Club, Athens, GA, USA 1/84
(Hindu Love Gods gig - Buck, Berry, Mills & Bryan Cook)
Friday's, Greensboro, NC, USA 1/84
40 Watt Club, Athens, GA, USA 2/84
(Hindu Love Gods gig. As per last month but plus Warren Zevon)
The Madhatter, Athens, GA, USA 8/3/84
The Madhatter, Athens, Ga, USA 9/3/84
Harvard University, Cambridge, MA, USA 23/3/84
The Paradiso, Amsterdam, Netherlands 8/4/84
Vrji Vloer, Utrecht, Netherlands 9/4/84
Dan Effenaar, Eindhoven, Netherlands (FM radio broadcast) 10/4/84
Exo-7, Rouen, France .... 17/4/84 ◆
West Side Club, Lyon, France 18/4/84
Clermont-Ferrand, France 19/4/84
L'Eldorado, Paris, France (FM radio broadcast in mono) .... 20/4/84 ◆
Fantasy Club, Birmingham, UK .... 24/4/84 ◆
The Gallery, Manchester, UK .... 25/4/84 ◆
(Includes: If I Had A Hammer, So You Want To Be A Rock'n'Roll Star, California Dreaming)
Warehouse, Leeds, UK .... 26/4/84 ◆
Nightmoves, Glasgow, Scotland, UK 27/4/84
The Carioca, Worthing, UK .... 29/4/84 ◆
(includes "Fever" and a rare version of "Voice Of Harold")
The Marquee, London, UK .... 30/4/84 ◆
The Marquee, London, UK .... 1/5/84 ◆
(Includes: I Can't Control Myself, Does Your Mother Know? and Skank).
"Saturday Live", BBC Radio, UK .... 5/5/84 ◆
(FM radio interview)
Capital Theatre, Passaic, NJ .... 9/6/84 ◆
(Includes guests Roger McGuinn & John Sebastian, part broadcast on MTV 'Rock Influences' TV Show)
WLIR FM radio broadcast, USA .... 13/6/84 ◆
(Interview with Bill Berry)

The Catalyst, Santa Cruz, CA, USA	17/6/84 ◆
Mission Theatre, Santa Barbara, CA, USA	18/6/84 ◆
'Rock Of The 80's' Cable TV Show, Palace Theatre, Hollywood, CA, USA	19/6/84 ◆
Delmar Fairgrounds, San Diego, CA, USA	20/6/84 ◆
Warfield Theatre, San Francisco, California, USA	22/6/84 ◆
(with special guests the Dream Syndicate)	
Mountain Air Festival, Calveros County, USA	23-4/6/89
(with Huey Lewis & The Cars)	
Portland, Oregon, USA	26/6/84
Music Hall, Seattle, Washington, DC, USA	27/6/84 ◆
(FM radio broadcast, also available as a radio promotional album and bootleg. Supported by The Dream Syndicate)	
Mardi Gras, Boise, ID	30/6/84 ◆
Rainbow Music Hall, Denver, CO, USA	3/7/84 ◆
Orpheum Theatre, Minneapolis, MN, USA	5/7/84
Entertainment Tonight, USA TV broadcast	6/7/84 ◆
Summerfest Rockstage, Milwaukee, WI, USA	6/7/84 ◆
Aragon Ballroom, Chicago, Ill, USA (FM radio broadcast)	7/7/84 ◆
Royal Oak Theatre, Detroit, MI, USA	8/7/84
Minett Hall, Rochester, NY, USA	11/7/84
Concert Hall, Toronto, Ontario, Canada	13/7/84
'The New Music' TV Show, City TV, Toronto, Ontario, Canada	13/7/84 ◆
(Interview with Mike Mills)	
Salty Dog Saloon, Buffalo, NY, USA	15/7/84 ◆
The Playpen, Wildwood, NJ, USA	16/7/84 ◆
The Orpheum, Boston, MA, USA	19/7/84 ◆
WCBN FM, Boston, MA, USA	19/7/84
(FM radio interview)	
The Agora, Hartford, CT, USA	20/7/84 ◆
Beacon Theatre, New York City, NY, USA	21-22/7/84 ◆
'Solid Gold Hits' TV Show, CBS TV, USA	26/7/84 ◆
War Memorial Auditorium, Greensboro, NC, USA	27/7/84
Fox Theatre, Atlanta, GA, USA	28/7/84
IRS 'Cutting Edge' , USA TV broadcast	29/7/84 ◆
New York City, NY, USA	19/8/84
(A Fleshtones gig, with Peter Buck joining the band for 'Wind Out')	
Pomona Valley Auditorium, Pomona, CA, USA	5/9/84
Greek Theatre, Los Angeles, CA, USA	6/9/84
Palace West, Pheonix, AZ, USA	8/9/84
Macky Auditorium, University Of Colorado, Boulder, CO, USA	11/9/84
Bowery, Oklahoma City, OK, USA	15/9/84
Park Centre, Charlotte, NC, USA	23/9/84
Page Auditorium, Duke University, Durham, NC, USA	25-26/9/84 ◆
(The Charlotte and two Durham gigs above were recorded by Reflection Studios for possible future release, as were 5 other shows from this period).	
University Of S. Florida, Tampa, FL, USA	28/9/84 ◆
Boca Raton, FL, USA	29/9/84
Gainsville, FL, USA	30/9/84
McAllister Auditorium, New Orleans, LA, USA	2/10/84
(with the dB's, as are the next 8 shows listed below)	
Oxford, MS, USA	3/10/84

Carbondale, IL, USA 5/10/84
Graham Chapel, St. Louis, MO, USA (soundboard) ....6/10/84 ◆
Dekalb, IL, USA 7/10/84
Hill Auditorium, Ann Arbor, MI, USA (soundboard) ....8./10/84 ◆
Charlottesvillle, VA, USA 11/10/84
University of Bridgeport, Bridgeport, CT, USA ....13/10/84 ◆
   (SET: Harborcoat, Talk About The Passion, Hyena, Seven
   Chinese Brothers, Driver 8, Pilgrimage,West Of The Fields,
   (Don't Go Back To) Rockville, Sitting Still, Old man Kensey,
   Gardening At Night, 9-9, Windout, So. Central Rain, Femme
   Fatale, Pretty Persuasion,Little America, Moon River, Camera,
   Time After Time,We Walk, Just A Touch, Radio Free Europe,
   Sloop John B.,I Can't Control Myself, Wild Thing, So You Want
   To Be A Rock'n'Roll Star, Carnival Of Sorts (Boxcars).
Fine Arts Centre, Amherst, MA, USA ....15/10/84 ◆
WMUA-FM Radio broadcast, Amherst, MA, USA ....15/10/84 ◆
   (Interview with Peter Buck)
Veterans Memorial Auditorium, Providence, Rhode Island, USA 16/10/84
Tower Theatre, Philadelphia, PA, USA ....17/10/84 ◆
The Circus, Oslo, Norway (FM radio broadcast) ....13/11/84 ◆
Rehearsal Hall, Tokyo, Japan 4/11/84
   (Show for journalists and students)
Waseda University, Tokyo, Japan 5/11/84
   (supported by Japanese band Bakufu Stom as are all Japanese
   gigs listed below)
Music School Auditorium, Japan 8/11/84
Yokohama University, Japan ....10/11/84 ◆
gymnasium, near Tokyo, Japan 11/11/84
Tiffany's, Newcastle, UK ....15/11/84 ◆
Caley Palace, Edinburgh, UK ....16/11/84 ◆
Manchester Polytechnic, Manchester, UK 17/11/84
Picadilly Radio, Manchester, UK ....17/11/84 ◆
   (FM radio interview with Peter Buck)
Royal Court, Liverpool, UK 18/11/84
Old Grey Whistle Test , London, UK ....20/11/84 ◆
   (Moon River/Pretty Persuasion, Old Man Kensey)
Rock City, Nottingham, UK ....21/11/84 ◆
   (Later used as BBC radio broadcast)
University Of East Anglia, Norwich, UK ....23/11/84 ◆
University Of Essex, Colchester, UK ....24/11/84 ◆
Birmingham University, Birmingham, UK ....26/11/84 ◆
Keisas, Leicester, UK ....27/11/84 ◆
New Ocean Club,Cardiff, Wales, UK 28/11/84
Queensway Hall, Dunstable, UK ....29/11/84 ◆
The Lyceum, London, UK ....2/12/84 ◆
   (Set includes "I Can Only Give You Everything" with Jeff
   Connolly of The Lyres)
SFX Centre, Dublin, Ireland (soundboard) ....4/12/84 ◆
   (REM are joined by Steve Wickham on '(Don't Go Back To) Rockville')
Civic Centre, Atlanta, GA, USA 31/12/84

1985

What a year. R.E.M. toured tirelessly throughout the USA, Canada and Europe, recorded the "Fables Of The Reconstruction" album which was released in June, and Peter Buck still found the time to tune Charlie Pickett's guitars one night in Tuscaloosa!

Uptown Lounge, Athens, GA, USA 12/2/85
  (REM play billed as Hornets Attack Victor Mature)
Moonshadow Club, Atlanta, GA, USA 18/2/85
John Keane Studios, Athens, GA, USA 19/2/85
  (REM record 16 demos for 'Fables Of The Reconstruction' LP)
Gibus Club, Paris, France 4/3/85
  (Peter Buck plays with the Fleshtones on 'Wind Out' & 'When The Night Falls')
Livingstone Studios, London, UK 3/85
  (Record 'Fables Of The Reconstruction' LP)
Dingwalls, Camden Lock, London, UK 15/3/85
  (A Robyn Hitchcock & The Egyptians gig with guest Peter Buck)
Radio City, New York, NY, USA 31/3/85
Waveform Media Rehearsal Studio, Atlanta, GA, USA 4/85
  (Rehearsed material for forthcoming shows)
Legion Field, Athens, GA, USA 22/4/85
  (Start of "Pre-Construction" tour. Also on the bill, that old Big Star, Alex Chilton)
Bucknell University, Lewisburg, PA, USA 25/4/85
Suny, Binghampton, NJ, USA 26/4/85
Brown University, Providence, Rhode Island, USA .... 27/4/85 ✦
Rutgers University, Piscathaway, NJ, USA .... 28/4/85 ✦
  (SET: Feeling Gravity's Pull, Harborcoat, Green Grow The Rushes,
  So. Central Rain, Good Advices, Hyena, Seven Chinese Brothers,
  Driver 8, Can't Get There From Here, Sitting Still, Maps & Legends,
  Talk About The Passion, Auctioneer, Old Man Kensey, Pretty
  Persuasion, When I Was Young, Little America, Have You Ever
  Seen The Rain, (Don't Go Back To) Rockville, Life And How To
  Live It, White Tornado, Theme From Two Steps Onward,
  Gardening At Night, 9-9, Windout).
Drew University, Madison, NJ, USA .... 30/4/85 ✦
New Athletic Centre, MIT, Cambridge, MA, USA .... 3/5/85 ✦
  (supported by The Neats)
Lansing Arena, Williamstown, MA, USA .... 4/5/85 ✦
Alumni Arena, Williams College, University Of Buffalo, NY, USA .... 5/5/85 ✦
McGaw Hall, North Western University, Chicago, IL, USA 8/5/85
Iowa City, Iowa, USA 9/5/85
Richmond, VA, USA 12/5/85
Stock Pavillion, Madison, WI, USA (soundboard) .... 15/5/85 ✦
Meredith College Amphitheatre, Raleigh, NC, USA .... 27/5/85 ✦
Drew University, Madison, NJ, USA 30/5/85
  (set includes version of Free's "All Right Now"!)
Milton Keynes Bowl, UK .... 22/6/85 ✦
  (supported U2)
Piccadilly Radio, Manchester, UK .... 23/6/85 ✦
  (FM radio interview with Peter Buck & Mike Mills)

Manchester International, Manchester, UK	24/6/85
Coasters, Edinburgh, Scotland, UK	25/6/85 ✦
Tiffany's, Newcastle, UK	26/6/85 ✦
Workroom, Warwick University, Coventry, UK	27/6/85 ✦

(After the REM set, Peter Buck also plays later with Green On Red who turn up at 2am for a belated appearance)

Capitol Radio, London, UK	28/6/85

(Interview with Peter Buck & Mike Mills)

Slane Castle, Dublin, Ireland	29/6/85
Piccadilly Radio, Manchester, UK	30/6/85 ✦

(FM radio phone-in interview with Mike Mills)

'The All American Rock 'n' Roll Weekend' TV Show, MTV, USA	5/7/85 ✦
'Saturday Live' BBC FM radio interview	6/7/85 ✦
Rock Torhout Festival, Belgium	6/7/85
Rock Werchter Festival, Belgium (FM broadcast)	7/7/85 ✦

(At the two gigs above, REM supported U2. Parts of the show were broadcast on 'Villa Tempo' TV show, Netherlands)

Portland, OR, USA	11/7/85

(Start of "Reconstruction 1" tour)

Paramount Theatre, Seattle, WA, USA	12/7/85 ✦

(with True West)

Commodore Ballroom, Vancouver, British Columbia, Canada	13/7/85
Cable TV, Vancouver, Canada (interview)	13/7/85
Edmonton, Alberta, Canada	15/7/85
Calgary, Alberta, Canada	16/7/85
WNYU FM, New York, USA	18/7/85

(FM radio interview)

Fresno, CA, USA	19/7/85
Community Theatre, Berkeley, CA, USA	20/7/85 ✦
Rockline (interview), Hollywood, CA, USA	22/7/85
Civic Auditorium, Santa Cruz, CA, USA	23/7/85 ✦
Santa Barbara, CA, USA	24/7/85
Open Air Theatre, San Diego, CA, USA	26/7/85 ✦
Greek Theatre, Hollywood, CA, USA	27/7/85 ✦

(Warren Zevon guests with REM)

Irvine Meadows Ampitheatre, Irvine, CA, USA	28/7/85 ✦
"Rock Today", WNEW-FM, New York, USA	29/7/85

(FM radio interview)

Palace West, Pheonix, AZ, USA	29/7/85
San Antonio, TX, USA	31/7/85
'Music Convoy' TV Show, WWF TV, Germany	7/85 ✦
Austin, TX, USA	1/8/85
Cullen Auditorium, Houston, TX, USA	2/8/85 ✦
Dallas, TX, USA	3/8/85
Minneapolis, MN, USA	5/8/85
Civic Centre Forum, St. Paul, MN, USA	6/8/85
U.I.C. Pavillion, Chicago, IL, USA	7/8/85
State Theatre, Kalamazoo, MI, USA	9/8/85
Fox Theatre, Detroit, MI, USA	10/8/85
Convention Centre Music Hall, Cleveland, OH, USA	12/8/85
Syria Mosque, Pittsburgh, PA	13/8/85

(supported by Three O'Clock)

Auditorium Theatre, Rochester, NY, USA	15/8/85 ✦
Concert Hall, Toronto, Ontario, Canada	16/8/85 ✦
"Much Music" TV (interview), Toronto, Ontario, Canada	16/8/85
"New Music" TV (interview), Toronto, Ontario, Canada	16/8/85
Barrymore's, Ottawa, Ontario, Canada	17/8/85 ✦

   (SET: Feeling Gravity's Pull, Radio Free Europe, Letter Never Sent, Pills, Can't Get There From Here, Seven Chinese Brothers, Laughing, Driver 8, Maps & Legends, Fall On Me, Have You Ever Seen The Rain, West Of The Fields, Auctioneer, Old man Kensey, Pretty Persuasion, Moral Kiosk, Life And How To Live It, Moon River, I Can't Control Myself, 1,000,000, I Can Only Give You Everything, Paint It Black, In The Year 2525, Smokin' In The Boys Room, Sweet Home Alabama, I'm Not Your Steppin' Stone, Secret Agent Man, The Lion Sleeps Tonight, God Save The Queen, Roadrunner, 20th Century Boy, Carnival Of Sorts (Boxcars)).(Phew!)

Montreal, Quebec, Canada	18/8/85
Cumberland County Civic Centre, Portland, Maine, USA	20/8/85
Walter Brown Arena, Boston, MA, USA	21/8/85
Leroy Theatre, Pawtucket, Rhode Island, USA	23/8/85 ✦
The Agora, Hartford, CT, USA	24/8/85
J.B. Scott's, Albany, NY, USA	25/8/85 ✦
Baltimore, MD, USA	26/8/85
Tower Theatre, Philadelphia, PA, USA	28/8/85 ✦
Washington, DC, USA	29/8/85
'Entertainment Tonight' TV Show, NBC TV, USA	29/8/85 ✦
Capitol Theatre, Passaic, NJ, USA	30/8/85 ✦
Radio City Music Hall, New York City, NY, USA	31/8/85 ✦
Milwaukee, Wisconsin, USA	8/85
WNEW FM, "Rock Today" (interview), New York, USA	2/9/85
The Paradiso, Amsterdam, Netherlands (FM radio broadcast)	1/10/85 ✦

   (Start of "Reconstruction II" tour)

Zeche, Bochum, West Germany	2/10/85 ✦

   (Broadcast on FM radio and shown on 'Rockpalast' TV show)

Arena, Rotterdam, Netherlands	3/10/85 ✦
Vooruit, Gent, Belgium	5/10/85 ✦
Batschkapp, Frankfurt, West Germany	6/10/85 ✦
Alabamahalle, Munich, West Germany	7/10/85 ✦

   (20 minutes broadcast on 'Live Concert' TV show)

West Berlin, West Germany	9/10/85
Markthalle, Hamburg, West Germany	10/10/85 ✦
Cologne, West Germany	11/11/85
Uni Aula, Saarbrucken, West Germany	13/10/85 ✦

   (Set includes cover of "Radar Love").

Eldorado, Paris, France	14/10/85 ✦
Salle Maliere, Lyon, France	15/10/85 ✦
Geneva, Switzerland	16/10/85
Alte Feuerwache, Mannheim, West Germany	18/10/85
Piccadilly Radio, Manchester, UK	20/10/85 ✦

   (FM radio interview)

The Ritz, Manchester, UK	20/10/85 ✦
The Roxy, Nottingham, UK	21/10/85 ✦
Octagon Centre, Sheffield, UK	22/10/85 ✦

Barrowlands, Glasgow, Scotland, UK	23/10/85	◆
The Tube, TV show, Newcastle, UK	25/10/85	◆
Royal Court, Liverpool, UK	26/10/85	◆
The Powerhouse, Birmingham, UK	27/10/85	◆
Hammersmith Palais, London, UK	28/10/85	◆
Hammersmith Palais, London, UK (soundboard)	29/10/85	◆

(Recorded for radio broadcast by Capital Radio - but not aired)

CU Events Centre, Boulder, CO, USA	2/11/85	

(Start of '[Reconstruction III]' tour)

Arts & Science Auditorium, Laramie, WY, USA	3/11/85	◆
Omaha, NE, USA	5/11/85	
Kansas City, MO	6/11/85	
University Of Indiana, Bloomington, IN, USA	8/11/85	◆
CMJ Awards show, Beacon Theatre, NY, USA	9/11/85	◆
Lexington, KY, USA	11/11/85	
Nashville, TN, USA	12/11/85	
Memphis, TN, USA	13/11/85	
Ames, IA, USA	15/11/85	

(supported by 10,000 Maniacs)

Radio Sheffield, Sheffield, UK	15/11/85	

(FM radio interview with Peter Buck)

Champaign, IL, USA	16/11/85	
Kiel Opera House, St. Louis, MO, USA	17/11/85	
New Orleans, LA, USA	19/11/85	
Tuscaloosa, AL, USA	21/11/85	
small club, Tuscaloosa, AL, USA	21/11/85	

(After their own gig REM's Peter Buck plays with Charlie Pickett & The MC3)

Talahassie, FL, USA	22/11/85	
Jacksonville, FL, USA	23/11/85	
James L. Knight Centre, Miami, FL, USA	24/11/85	
Bayfront Theatre, St. Petersburg, FL, USA	26/11/85	◆
Civic Centre, Savannah, GA, USA	27/11/85	
Fox Theatre, Atlanta, GA, USA	29-30/11/85	◆

(supported by the Minutemen & Jason & The Scorchers)

Civic Centre, Raleigh, NC, USA	2/12/85	◆
Boone, NC, USA	3/12/85	
Chrysler Auditorium, Norfolk, VA, USA	4/12/85	◆
The Mosque, Richmond, VA, USA	5/12/85	
Washington & Lee University, Lexington, VA, USA	6/12/85	
Reynolda Auditorium, Winston-Salem, NC, USA	8/12/85	◆
Radford College, Radford, VA, USA	9/12/85	
Veterans Memorial Auditorium, Columbus, OH, USA	10/12/85	
Columbia, SC, USA	11/12/85	
Park Centre, Charlotte, NC, USA	13/12/85	
Augusta, GA, USA	14/12/85	
The World, New York City, NY, USA	20/12/85	

(not an REM show, but a Coyote Records Christmas party celebrating the release of that label's excellent "Luxury Condos" compilation album. The entertaiment featured a rare appearance of the Full Time Men, featuring Peter Buck and most of The Fleshtones. The set includes the Men's "Way Down South" & "One More Time", REM's "Windout" and the Fleshtones' own "Critical List").

Indianapolis, Indiana, USA	12/85	

1986

For the first time since 1982, R.E.M. confine the year's touring to the USA and Canada. Michael plays gigs with the Golden Palominos, while Mike Mills and Bill Berry take to the boards with the Corn Cob Webs. "Life's Rich Pageant", R.E.M.'s fourth full album was released in July.

Lucy Cobb Chapel, Athens, GA, USA 1/86
   (REM filmed here performing for the video 'Athens, GA, Inside-Out')
The Ritz, New York City, NY, USA .... 9/1/86 ♦
   (Not an REM gig, but one by the Golden Palominos - Michael Stipe joins the band to perform live versions of the 3 tracks on which he appears on the "Visions Of Excess" album, plus a cover of a Richard Thompson song. Other gigs with the Golden Palominos include: San Francisco 24/1/86, Los Angeles 26/1/86, Daytona Beach 28/1/86 and the Moonshadow in Atlanta 29/1/86)
40 Watt Club, Athens, GA, USA .... 20/1/86 ♦
   (A benefit gig in respect of D. Boon, late of The Minutemen. This REM gig included an acoustic set, a Hindu Love Gods section also featuring Bryan Cooke deputising for Michael Stipe who reappeared for an acapella version of Bill Withers' classic "Ain't No Sunshine").
John Keane Studios, Athens, GA, USA 2/86
   (Recorded a demo of 'Fall On Me')
Athens, GA, USA 8/3/86
   (not an REM gig but one by The Corn Cob Webs, Mike Mills and Bill Berry's 'hobby' band).
John Keane Studios, Athens, GA, USA 3/86
   (Recorded demos for 'Life's Rich Pageant')
Belmont Mall Studios, Bloomington, Illinois, USA 4-5/86
   (Recorded 'Life's Rich Pageant')
WLIR-FM/WNYU-FM/K-Rock (interviews), New York, USA 19/8/86
WLUP (interview), Chicago, IL, USA 20/8/86
Oak Mountain Amphitheatre, Birmingham, AL, USA .... 5/9/86 ♦
University Of Indiana, Bloomington, IN, USA .... 6/9/86 ♦
WNEW, "Rock Today" (interview), New York, USA 6/9/86
Taft Theatre, Cincinnati, OH, USA 7/9/86
Memorial Auditorium, Louisville, KY, USA 8/9/86
Grand Ol' Opry, Nashville, TN, USA .... 10/9/86 ♦
Municipal Auditorium, Jackson, MS, USA 11/9/86
Saenger Theatre, New Orleans, LA, USA 12/9/86
Mudd Island Amphitheatre, Memphis, TN, USA .... 13/9/86 ♦
   (supported by Fetchin' Bones)
Robinson Auditorium, Little Rock, AR, USA 15/9/86
Music Hall, Oklahoma City, OK, USA 17/9/86
The Coliseum, Austin, TX, USA 18/9/86
Southern Star Amphitheatre, Houston, TX, USA .... 19/9/86 ♦
The Bandshell, Dallas State Fairgrounds, Dallas, TX, USA 20/9/86
Pan American Centre, Las Cruces, NM, USA 22/9/86
Mesa Amphitheatre, Mesa, AZ, USA 23/9/86
   (Supported by Guadalcanal Diary)

Pacific Amphitheatre, Cosa Mesa, CA, USA	24/9/86
Greek Theatre, Berkeley, CA, USA	26/9/86
County Bowl, Sanat Barbara, CA, USA	27/9/86
UCSD Gym, San Diego, CA, USA	28/9/86
Universal Amphitheatre, Universal City, Los Angeles, CA, USA	30/9/86 ✦
Oakland Coliseum, Oakland, CA, USA	1/10/86 ✦
Holt Centre, Eugene, OR, USA	2/10/86
Civic Auditorium, Portland, OR, USA	3/10/86
Paramount Theatre, Seattle, WA, USA	4/10/86
War Memorial Arena, Vancouver, British Columbia, Canada	5/10/86
Fairgrounds Coliseum, Salt Lake City, UT, USA	7/10/86
CU Events Centre, Boulder, CO, USA	9/10/86 ✦
Pershing Auditorium, Lincoln, NE, USA	10/10/86
Memorial Hall, Kansas City, MO, USA	11/10/86
Kiel Opera House, St. Louis, MO, USA	12/10/86
Roy Wilkins Auditorium, St. Paul, MN, USA	14/10/86
Hncher Auditorium, Iowa City, IO, USA	15/10/86
Oriental Theatre, Milwaukee, WI, USA	17/10/86
Grand Centre, Grand Rapids, MI, USA	18/10/86
Viceroy Pavillion, University Of Illinois, Chicago, IL, USA	19/10/86
Chick Evans Fieldhouse, Dekalb, IL, USA	21/10/86

(Gary Zekley, original member of the Clique and writer of "Superman" joins REM onstage for that song).

Fox Theatre, Detroit, MI, USA	22/10/86
Public hall, Cleveland, OH, USA	23/10/86

(Richard Thompson joins the band onstage)

Syria Mosque, Pittsburgh, PA, USA	24/10/86 ✦
Shea's Theatre, Buffalo, NY, USA	26/10/86
Massey Hall, Toronto, Canada	27/10/86 ✦

(Natalie Merchant guest with REM)

Montreal, Canada	29/10/86
University Of New Hampshire Fieldhouse, Durham, NH, USA	30/10/86
UVM Patrick Gym, Burlington, VT, USA	31/10/86
Boston, MA, USA	1/11/86
Wang Centre, Boston, MA, USA	2/11/86 ✦
Hartford, Connecticut, USA	4/11/86
Felt Forum, New York City, NY, USA	6/11/86 ✦

(REM are joined by ex-Clique member Gary Zekley for 'Superman')

Felt Forum, New York City, NY, USA	7/11/86 ✦
The Coliseum, New Haven, CT, USA	8/11/86 ✦
Spectrum Showcase, Philadelphia, PA, USA	9/11/86

(Supported by Mitch Easter's band Let's Active also next 13 shows listed)

William & Mary Hall, Williamsburg, VA, USA	10/11/86
Washington DC, VA, USA	11/11/86
Charlottesville, VA, USA	12/11/86
Cameron Indoor Stadium, Duke University, Durham, NC, USA	15/11/86
Wilmington, NC, USA	16/11/86

(Ex-Mountain drummer Corky Laing joins the band onstage)

Township Hall, Columbia, SC, USA	17/11/86
Georgia Southern College, Statesboro, GA, USA	19/11/86
Civic Auditorium, Jacksonville, FL, USA	20/11/86

Bayfront Arena, St. Petersburg, FL, USA 21/11/86
    (Roger McGuinn joins the band onstage)
James L. Knight Centre, Miami, FL, USA 22/11/86
Fox Theatre, Atlanta, GA, USA 24-26/11/86
(unknown studio) USA 28/11/86
    (recorded 'Romance')

1987

Apart from a couple of European shows, R.E.M. confined their personal appearances to the USA again this year. Two albums were released in 1987, first the compilation of oddities and B-sides, "Dead Letter Office" in April, and, five months later "Document".

40 Watt Club, Athens, GA, USA .... 19/1/87   ✦
    (Gig featuring Michael Stipe + ??)
Uptown Lounge, Athens, GA, USA 25/3/87
    (REM support Charlie Pickett and the MC3!!)
McCabe's Guitar Shop, Santa Monica, CA, USA .... 24/5/87   ✦
    (was taped, some songs used for B-sides etc. A benefit gig also featuring Steve
    Wynn and Natalie Merchant)
40 Watt Club, Athens, GA, USA .... 19/8/87   ✦
40 Watt Club, Athens, GA, USA 3/9/87
John Keane Studios, Athens, GA, USA 4/9/87
    (Recorded 'Last Date')
Hammersmith Odeon, London, UK .... 12/9/87   ✦
    (Robyn Hitchcock guests with REM. Supported by 10,000 Maniacs)
Muziekcentrum, Utrecht, Netherlands (FM radio broadcast) .... 14/9/87   ✦
'Kippevel' TV Show, Vara TV, Utrecht, Netherlands .... 14/9/87   ✦
    (interview)
La Pigalle, Paris, France 16/9/87
Tor 3, Dusseldorf, Germany 18/9/87
Knoxville, TN, USA 1/10/87
    (Start of "Work" tour, this and next 18 gigs below supported by 10,000 Maniacs)
Clemson University, Clemson, SC, USA 2/10/87
Duke University, Durham, NC, USA 3/10/87
Duke University, Durham, NC, USA 4/10/87
Radio City Music Hall, New York City, NY, USA 6/10/87
Radio City Music Hall, New York City, NY, USA 7/10/87
William & Mary College, Williamsburg, VA, USA 9/10/87
Patriot Centre, Fairfax, VA, USA 10/10/87
State College, PA, USA 11/10/87
UVA, Charlottesville, VA, USA 13/10/87
Charleston, WV, USA 14/10/87
    (Set: Finest Worksong, These Days, Welcome To The Occupation, Disturbance
    At The Heron House, Exhuming McCarthy, Orange Crush, Feeling Gravity's Pull,
    King Of Birds, I Believe, Fire Place, Driver 8, Cuyahoga, Superman, Auctioneer,
    Odd Fellows Local 151, It's The End Of The World As We Know It,
    Begin The Begin, Strange, Lighnin' Hopkins, Fall On Me, Life And How To Live It,

Midnight Blue, 1,000,000, The One I Love, Just A Touch).
Spectrum Showcase, Philadelphia, PA, USA	16/10/87
New Haven, CT, USA	17/10/87
Worcester, MA, USA	18/10/87
Performing Arts Centre, Providence, Rhode Island, USA	19/10/87
Portland, Maine, USA	21/10/87
New Brunswick, New Jersey, USA	22/10/87
Pittsburgh, PA, USA	23/10/87
Columbus, OH, USA	24/10/87
East Lansing, MI, USA	26/10/87
Lafayette, IN, USA	27/10/87
Ann Arbor, MI, USA	29/10/87
Oxford, OH, USA	30/10/87
Davenport, Iowa, USA	31/10/87
'Week In Rock' TV Show, MTV, USA	10/87 ✦
Minneapolis, MN, USA	2/11/87
Madison, WI, USA	3/11/87
(this and next 19 gigs below supported by The dB's)	
University Of Chicago Pavillion, Chicago, IL, USA	4-5/11/87 ✦
Champaign, IL, USA	7/11/87
Kansas City, MO, USA	8/11/87
Lincoln, NE, USA	9/11/87
St. Louis, MO	10/11/87
Los Angeles, CA, USA	11/11/87
Oakland Coliseum, Oakland, CA, USA	13/11/87
Holt Centre, Irving, CA, USA	14/11/87
Universal Amphitheatre, Los Angeles, CA, USA	15/11/87 ✦
Tempe, AZ, USA	16/11/87
Dallas, TX, USA	18/11/87
Austin, TX, USA	19/11/87
Houston, TX, USA	20/11/87
Oxford, MS, USA	22/11/87
Auburn, AL, USA	23/11/87
Fox Theatre, Atlanta, GA, USA	24-25/11/87
Fox Theatre, Atlanta, GA, USA	27-28/11/87

1988

Not much live activity this year as REM concentrated on recording their 'Green' album which was released in November by Warner Brothers, just after the appearance of the IRS compilation "Eponymous". Nevertheless, all of the band did manage to find gigs with other likely parties...

John Keane Studios, Athens, GA, USA	2-3/88
(Recording demos for 'Green')	
Athens, GA, USA	25/3/88 ✦
(Peter Buck/Robyn Hitchcock gig)	

Atlanta, GA, USA .... 11/5/88 ◆
  (Gig by the 'Southern Gentlemen' aka Berry, Mills & Buck with Roger McGuinn preserved on the "Byrds Fly South" bootleg)
Ardent Studios, Memphis, TN, USA 5-7/88
  (Recordings for 'Green')
Bearsville Studios, Woodstock, NY, USA 7/88
  (Recorded 'Turn You Inside Out' and did mixing for 'Green')
40 Watt Club, Athens, GA, USA 8/7/88
Pier 84, New York City, NY, USA 8/9/88
  (10,000 Maniacs gig featuring guest appearance by Michael Stipe)
Athens Music Festival, Fairgrounds, Athens, GA, USA .... 25/9/88 ◆
  (The Indigo Girls with Michael Stipe)
Athens, GA, USA 13/10/88
  (REM present Warner Brothers with 'Green', live by Satellite).
'The New Music' TV Show, City TV, Toronto, Ontario, Canada .... 11/88 ◆
  (interview)

1989

For the first year since 1982, no new R.E.M. album was released. Most of the year was consumed by the massive 'Green World Tour', which also saw the addition of Peter Holsapple to the line-up. Despite the heavy tour schedule Peter Buck and Mike Mills still manage to play extra gigs as part of Worse Case Scenario and Nigel & The Crosses. All is revealed below...

Rehearse Too Much Studios, Atlanta, GA, USA 1/89
  (Rehearsals for forthcoming 'Green World Tour')
The Basement, Atlanta, GA, USA 19/1/89
40 Watt Club, Athens, GA, USA 23/1/89
  (Video for 'Turn You Inside Out' recorded on this occasion)
MZA Stadium, Tokyo, Japan .... 26-27/1/89 ◆
  (Start of the "Green" world tour which continues throughout 1989. All gigs feature Peter Holsapple as a 'fifth member')
Town Hall, Christchurch, New Zealand 2/2/89
  (supported by the Go-Betweens, as are the next eight gigs)
Town Hall, Wellington, New Zealand 3/2/89
Logan Campbell Centre, Auckland, New Zealand 4/2/89
Concert Hall, Perth, Australia 8-9/2/89
The Barton Theatre, Adelaide, Australia 11/2/89
Festival Hall, Melbourne, Australia 12/2/89
Festvial Hall, Brisbane, Australia 15/2/89
Hordern Pavillion, Sydney, Australia 17/2/89
Louisville, KY, USA 1/3/89
Carbondale, IL, USA 2/3/89
St. Louis Arena, St. Louis, MO, USA 3/3/89
  (supported by Robyn Hitchcock & The Egyptians)
Kansas City, MO, USA 4/3/89

Cubby The Bear's, Chicago, IL, USA .... 5/3/89 ◆
   *(The first Nigel & The Crosses gig featuring Peter Buck, Peter Holsapple
   and Robyn Hitchcock - may have been billed as 'Worse Case Scenario')*
Rosemont Horizon, Chicago, IL, USA 6/3/89
Iowa City, IA, USA 7/3/89
MET Centre, Minneapolis, MN, USA 8/3/89
First Avenue, Minneapolis, MN, USA 8/3/89
   *(Another late night set by 'Worst Case Scenario' aka Nigel & The Crosses
   aka Peter Buck, Robyn Hitchcock & The Egyptians and Mike Mills)*
Omaha, NE, USA 10/3/89
Argo Arena, Sacramentro, CA, USA 13/3/89
Oakland Coliseum, Oakland, CA, USA 14/3/89
The Forum, Los Angeles, CA, USA 15/3/89
Sports Arena, San Diego, CA, USA 16/3/89
ASU Activities Centre, Tempe, AZ, USA 18/3/89
San Antonio, TX, USA 20/3/89
Austin, TX, USA 21/3/89
Dallas, TX, USA 22/3/89
Houston, TX, USA 23/3/89
Shreveport, Louisianna, USA 25/3/89
Lakefront Arena, New Orleans, LA, USA .... 27/3/89 ◆
Birmingham. AL, USA 28/3/89
Memphis, TN, USA 30/3/89
Murphreesboro, TN, USA 31/3/89
'100 Minutes' TV Show, Much Music TV, Toronto, Ontario, Canada .... 1/4/89 ◆
The Omni, Atlanta, GA, USA 1-2/4/89
   (supported by the Inigo Girls at these two shows)
Cicinnatti, OH, USA 4/4/89
The Coliseum, Cleveland, OH, USA 6/4/89
The Coliseum, Morgantown, WV, USA 7/4/89
The Centrum, Worcester, MA, USA 9/4/89
Madison Square Gardens, New York City, NY, USA 10/4/89
War Memorial Auditorium, Syracuse, NY, USA 11/4/89
Maple Leaf Gardens, Toronto, Ontario, Canada 12/4/89
Montreal Forum, Montreal, Quebec, Canada 14/4/89
Civic Centre, Portland, ME, USA 15/4/89
Boston Gardens, Boston, MA, USA .... 16/4/89 ◆
Capitol Centre, Largo, MD, USA 18/4/89
'MTV News' TV Show, MTV, USA .... 18/4/89 ◆
   (interview)
The Spectrum Showcase, Philadelphia, PA, USA 20/4/89
Richmond Coliseum, Richmond, VA, USA 21/4/89
Dean Smith Centre, Chapel Hill, NC, USA 22/4/89
The Coliseum, Charlotte, NC, USA 23/4/89
Carolina Coliseum, Columbia, SC, USA 25/4/89
Civic Centre, Savannah, GA, USA 26/4/89
The Sun Dome, Tampa, FL, USA 28/4/89
Miami Arena, Miami, FL, USA .... 29/4/89 ◆
Orlando Arena, Orlando, Florida, USA .... 30/4/89 ◆
   (FM Radio broadcast)
'Rapido' TV Show, BBC2 TV, UK .... 4/89 ◆
Leon County Civic Centre, Talahassie, FL, USA 2/5/89

Von Braun Arena, Huntsville, AL, USA	3/5/89
'Schachtop' TV Show, Germany	8/5/89 ◆
Dusseldorf, West Germany	9/5/89
Phillips Hall, Munich, West Germany (FM Broadcast)	10/5/89
Bieldfeld, West Germany *(Cancelled due to Bill Berry being ill)*	12/5/89
Frankfurt, West Germany *(Cancelled due to Bill Berry being ill)*	13/5/89
Hamburg, West Germany *(Cancelled due to Bill Berry being ill)*	14/5/89
Pink Pop Festival, Landgraaf, Netherlands (FM broadcast)	15/5/89 ◆
'Zomerock' TV Show, Vara TV, Netherlands	15/5/89 ◆
De Montfort Hall, Leicester, UK	17/5/89 ◆

(supported by the Blue Aeroplanes - as are the next eight gigs)

Newport Centre, Newport, Gwent, Wales, UK	18/5/89
Guild Hall, Portsmouth, UK	19/5/89 ◆

(SET: Pop Song 89, Exhuming McCarthy, Pilgrimage, Turn You Inside Out, Disturbance At The Heron House, Orange Crush, Cuyahoga, Feeling Gravity's Pull, Driver 8, World Leader Pretend, Begin The Begin, White Tornado, Strange, Get Up, Life And How To Live It, It's The End Of The World And I Fell Fine, Stand, Academy Fight Song, You Are The Everything, Summertime, Finest Worksong, King Of Birds, Sitting Still, Perfect Circle, After Hours).

Royal Court, Liverpool, UK	21/5/89 ◆
Royal Concert Hall, Nottigham, UK	22/5/89 ◆
Playhouse Theatre, Edinburgh, Scotland, UK	23/5/89 ◆
Barrowlands, Glasgow, Scotland, UK	24/5/89 ◆
City Hall, Newcastle, UK	26/5/89
Apollo Theatre, Manchester, UK	27/5/89
The Borderline, London, UK	28/5/89 ◆

(The legendary Nigel & The Crosses gig - featuring Peter Buck, Robyn Hitchcock and the Egyptians, Peter Holsapple, Mike Mills, Billy Bragg, Glen Tilbrook & others)

Hammersmith Odeon, London, UK	29/5/89 ◆

(SET 28/5: Pop Song 89, Welcome To The Occupation, Turn You Inside Out, Fall On Me, Orange Crush, Disturbance At The Heron House, Feeling Gravity's Pull, King Of Birds, World Leader Pretend, Begin The Begin, Rotary 10, Pretty Persuasion, Get Up, Auctioneer, It's The End Of The World As We Know It, Stand, Low(uneleased new song), Crazy, You Are The Everything, Summertime, Finest Worksong, Perfect Circle, After Hours).

Hammersmith Odeon, London, UK	30/5/89 ◆
NEC, Birmingham, UK	31/5/89 ◆
Provinssirock Festival, Senajoki, Finland	4/6/89 ◆
Gota Leja, Stockholm, Sweden	6/6/89
Oslo, Norway	7/6/89
Oslo, Norway	8/6/89
Saga, Copenhagen, Denmark	9/6/89
BBC Radio 1, 'Saturday Sequence'	10/6/89 ◆

(Interview with Peter Buck)

Metropol, Berlin, Germany	11/6/89
Zurich, Switzerland	14/6/89
Palatrussardi, Milan, Italy	15/6/89 ◆
'Top Of The Pops' TV Show, BBC1 TV, UK	15/6/89
Palasport, Bologne, Italy	16/6/89 ◆

(some tracks from the above on 'The Dream' bootleg CD)

Palasport, Perugia, Italy	17/6/89 ◆

('Green World Tour' bootleg CD taped at above show)

Peter Buck & Michael Stipe. Photo by Marty Perez.

Paris, France	20/6/89
'Our Common Future' TV Show, A&E TV, Canada	22/6/89 ◆
(via satellite link-up)	
Wembley Arena, London, UK	22/6/89 ◆
(supported by Throwing Muses)	
RDS Simmonscourt, Dublin, Ireland	24/6/89
Grosse Freheit, Hamburg, Germany	27/6/89 ◆
Komgresshalle, Frankfurt, Germany	28/6/89
Circus Krone, Cologne, Germany	29/6/89
Rock Torhout Festival, Belgium	1/7/89 ◆
Rock Werchter Festival, Belgium	2/7/89 ◆
'Notte Rock' TV Show, RAI 1 TV, Italy	14/7/89 ◆
(TV interview with Stipe & Mills)	
'REM Special TV Show, Video Musica TV, Italy	18/7/89 ◆
Market Square, Indianapolis, IN, USA	8/9/89
Pine Knob, Clarkston, MI, USA	9/9/89
Civic Centre, Pittsburgh, PA, USA	10/9/89
Memorial Auditorium, Buffalo, New York, USA	12/9/89
(Supported by Throwing Muses)	
Civic Centre, Hartford, CT, USA	13/9/89 ◆
Great Woods, Mansfield, MA, USA	15-16/9/89
Mann Music Centre, Philadelphia, PA, USA	17/9/89 ◆
Meadowlands, East Rutherford, NJ, USA	19/9/89
Nassau Coliseum, Uniondale, NY, USA	20/9/89
Merriweather Post, Columbia, MD, USA	22-23/9/89
University Of Dayton, Dayton, OH, USA	26/9/89
Assembly Hall, Champaign, IL, USA	27/9/89
Notre Dame, South Bend, IN, USA	29/9/89
Alpine Valley, East Troy, WI, USA	30/9/89
'Post Modern' TV Show, MTV, USA	9/89
(TV interview with Michael Stipe)	
Hilton Coliseum, Ames, IO, USA	1/10/89
Devaney Sports Centre, Lincoln, NE, USA	3/10/89
McNichols Sports Arena, Denver, CO, USA	5/10/89
Salt Palace, Salt Lake City, UT	7/10/89
University Centre, Boise, ID, USA	8/10/89
Beasley Coliseum, Pullman, WA, USA	10/10/89
Seattle Centre, Seattle, WA, USA	11/10/89
Coliseum, Portland, OR, USA	13/10/89 ◆
Pacific National Exhibition, Vancouver, BC, Canada	14/10/89
'Arsenia Hall' TV Show, Fox TV, USA	17/10/89 ◆
Pacific Amphitheatre, Costa Mesa, CA, USA	18/10/89
Pavillion, Concord, CA, USA	20/10/89
Shoreline Amphitheatre, Mountain VIew, CA, USA	21/10/89
Compton Terrace, Pheonix, AZ, USA	24/10/89
Community Centre Arena, Tuscon, AZ, USA	25/10/89
Pan Am Centre, Las Cruces, NM, USA	26/10/89
Myriad Arena, Oklahoma City, OK, USA	28/10/89
Louisiana State Assembly, Baton Rouge, LA, USA	30/10/89 ◆
Leon County Arena, Tallahassee, FL, USA	1/11/89
University Of Tennessee Arena, Chattanooga, TN, USA	3/11/89
Thompson Boling Arena, Knoxville, TN, USA	4/11/89

Rupp Arena, Lexington, KY, USA 5/11/89
Civic Centre, Roanoke, VA, USA 7/11/89
Hampton Coliseum, Hampton, VA, USA 8/11/89
Coliseum, Greensboro, NC, USA ...... 10/11/89 ◆
   (Gig recorded. 'Bucketfull Of Brains' version of 'Academy Fight Song' recorded here)
Coliseum, Macon, GA, USA 11/11/89
Fox Theatre, Atlanta, GA, USA 12/11/89
Fox Theatre, Atlanta, GA, USA 13/11/89

1990

During this year REM spent time recording and mixing the 'Out Of Time' album in various studios (including Bearsville in Woodstock, NY; John Keane Studios in Athens, GA and Prince's Paisley Park, Minnesota). They still found a little time for the odd gig or guest appearance though....

40 Watt Club, Athens, GA, USA 5/4/90
   (10th anniversary gig)
9.30 Club, Washington, DC, USA 20/4/90
   (A 10,000 Maniacs gig, featuring a guest appearance by Michael Stipe)
Earth Day Concert, USA 22/4/90
   (Stipe, Buck, 10,000 Maniacs, Indigo Girls & Billy Bragg!)
Atlanta, GA, USA 26/5/90
   (with Kilkenny Cats, Love Tractor)
Big Day Festival, Glasgow, Scotland, UK 3/6/90
   (A Billy Bragg gig - featuring an appearance by Michael Stipe & Natalie Merchant)
40 Watt Club, Athens, GA, USA 31/7/90
   (Above gig features Buck, Mills & Berry plus guest vocalist)
40 Watt Club, Athens, GA, USA 19/12/90
   (A set by Peter Buck, Robyn Hitchcock and Kevn Kinney)

1991

This year saw the release of the "Out Of Time" - R.E.M.'s first new album release since 1988. Despite remaining unwilling to tour, R.E.M. did manage a few low-key appearances at small venues, together with TV and radio sessions, in order to promote their new album.

Studio II, NDR Radio, Hamburg, Germany ...... 5/3/91 ◆
   (Recording of live acoustic set: World Leader Pretend, Half A World Away, Belong, Fretless, Radio Song, You Are The Everything, Losing My Religion. Broadcast 13/4/91)
KDGE radio, Dallas, TX, USA ...... 7/3/91 ◆
   (Interview with Peter Buck)
Bulletsound Studios, Nederhorst Den Berg, Netherlands ...... 12/3/91 ◆

(Recording of acoustic set for VARA Radio, Netherlands: World leader Prtend, You Are The Everything, Fretless, Radio Song, Losing My Religion, Belong, Love Is All Around)
VPRO Radio, Netherlands .... 13/3/91 ◆
(Interview with Peter Buck recorded 12/3/91)
BBC Radio 1, 'Nicky Campbell Show' London, UK .... 13/3/91 ◆
(Live acoustic set and interview by Nicky Campbell)
BBC TV 'Late Show', London, UK .... 14/3/91 ◆
(Live acoustic set)
The Borderline, Charing Cross Rd, London, UK .... 14/3/91 ◆
(Bingo Hand Job gig featuring REM, Peter Holsapple, Billy Bragg, Robyn Hitchcock, Andy Metcalfe, Morris Windsor)
The Borderline, Charing Cross Rd, London, UK .... 15/3/91 ◆
(2nd Bingo Hand Job gig - as above minus Andy Metcalfe. The Bingos were supported by the Chickasaw Mudd Puppies who were joined briefly my Michael Stipe)
Veronica Radio, Netherlands .... 15/3/91 ◆
(Interview with Michael Stipe & Mike Mills recorded 12/3/91)
Villa Lux, RTL4 (TV broadcast) .... 20/3/91 ◆
(interview with Peter Buck & Bill Berry)
Rapido TV Show, BBC2 TV, UK .... 20/3/91 ◆
Shocking Club, Milan, Italy .... 22/3/91 ◆
(Gig for journalists, media types, tc, only. Broadcast on Video Musica TV, Italy)
'REM Special' , Video Musica TV, Italy .... 22/3/91 ◆
(see above entry)
VPRO TV, Netherlands .... 24/3/91 ◆
(Interview and acoustic set recorded 12/3/91)
'Friday Night At The Dome', Channel 4 TV show, UK .... 3/91 ◆
'Rockopop' TV Show, TVE 2, Spain .... 3/91 ◆
(Interview)
'Metropolis' TV Show, TVE 2, Spain .... 3/91 ◆
(Interview)
'Rockline', Hollywood, CA, USA .... 1/4/91 ◆
(Interview & 4 acoustic songs)
KCRW-FM Radio 'Snap' show, Santa Monica, CA, USA .... 3/4/91 ◆
'(Live studio set featuring many unusual covers, TV theme tunes etc)
Unplugged' TV Show, MTV, Chelsea Studios, NY, USA .... 10/4/91 ◆
WNEW-FM radio, New York City, NY, USA .... 12/4/91 ◆
(interview with Michael Stipe & Mike Mills)
'Saturday Night Live' TV Show, NBC TV, USA .... 13/4/91 ◆
Pepsi's New Music Experience, USA .... 21/4/91 ◆
(Interview with Peter Buck)
105 Live, San Francisco, CA, USA .... 23/4/91 ◆
(interview with Peter Buck & Mike Mills)
KRQR-FM radio, San Francisco, CA, USA .... 23/4/91 ◆
(Interview with Peter Buck and Mike Mills)
'Mountain Stage' radio show, Capitol Theatre, Charleston,
West Virginia, USA .... 28/4/91 ◆
(Recorded for broadcast)
'The Hot Seat' TV Show, MTV, USA .... 4/91 ◆
(Interview)
East Sound Studio 1, Toronto, Ontario, Canada .... 9/5/91 ◆

(Interview & live acoustic session: World Leader Pretend, Half A World Away, Radio Song, Love Is All Around, Losing My Religion, Fretless).
40 Watt Club, Athens, GA, USA .... 15/6/91 ◆
  (REM played billed as 'William')
40 Watt Club, Athens, GA, USA 7/91
  (A Feelies gig - they were joined by Stipe & Berry for 'See No Evil')
MTV Music Video Awards, USA .... 5/9/91 ◆

1992

Much of the early part of the year was taken up with the recording and mixing of the "Automatic For The People" album, which was released worldwide in the first week of October. As may be deduced from the meagre list below, the band are maintaining their 'no touring' stance.

40 Watt Club, Athens, GA, USA 31/1/92
Brit Awards '92, Hammersmith Odeon, London 12/2/92
Grammy Awards, Rock City Music Hall, New York City, NY, USA 2/92
The Powerhaus, Islington, London, UK .... 17/10/92 ◆
  (Although rumoured by the press to be a 'secret' REM gig, this benefit for
  refugee relief in Bosnia featured Robyn Hitchcock, various Egyptians/Soft Boys
  and... Peter Buck who played guitar for about half of the 90 minute set)
GLR Radio, London, UK .... 18/10/92 ◆
  (Interview with Peter Buck & Mike Mills)

VIDEOS

Four REM videos are currently commercially available: "REM Succumbs" and "Pop Screen" are both basically collections of promo clips - the former also includes the 20 minute "Left Of Reckoning" which utilises the songs from the first side of the "Reckoning" album as a soundtrack. The 85 minute "Tourfilm", documents the 1989 "Green" world tour and features extensive live footage from US concerts. "This Film Is On" is a collection of both and promo videos.

In addition to these three releases REM are also included, both playing and being interviewed in the "Athens G.A. - Inside Out" video (together with other artists).

In a non-musical vein, Michael Stipe appears in an independent film short, directed by Robert Longo, entitled "Arena Brains".

☐ **"REM Succumbs"** **A&M Video 61710 (VHS)** **1987**
(Features promo videos: Radio Free Europe, So. Central Rain (I'm Sorry), Left Of Reckoning, Can't Get There From Here, Driver 8, Life And How To Live It, Feeling Gravity's Pull, Fall On Me).
☐ "REM Succumbs" A&M Video 21710 (Betamax) 1987
☐ "REM Succumbs" Polygram Video LED 80192 1991
(mid-price re-issue)

☐ **"Pop Screen"** **Warner Brothers 7599-38156-3** **1990**
(Features promo videos: The One I Love, It's The End Of The World As We Know It (And I Feel Fine), Finest Worksong, Talk About The Passion, Orange Crush, Stand, Turn You Inside Out, Pop Song 89, Get Up).

☐ **"Tourfilm"** **Warner Brothers 7599-38184-3** **1990**
(Features live recordings from the 'Green World Tour' 7-13/11/89:
Stand, The One I Love, So. Central Rain (I'm Sorry)(partial), These Days, Turn You Inside Out, World Leader pretend, Feeling Gravity's Pull, I Believe, I Remember California, Get Up, It's The End Of The World As We Know It (And I Feel Fine), Pop Song '89, Belong (partial), Fall On Me, You Are The Everything, Begin The Begin, King Of Birds, Low (partial), Finest Worksong, Perfect Circle, After Hours).

☐ **"This Film Is On"** **Warner Brothers 7599-38254-3** **1991**
(Features promo and live videos: Losing My Religion, Shiny Happy People, Near Wild Heaven, Radio Song,, Love Is All Around (liveon MTV 'Unplugged' 10/4/91), Losing My Religion (liveon 'The Late Show' BBC TV, UK 14/3/91), Low, Belong (promo video with live recording from the Coliseum, Greensboro, NC, USA), Half A World Away, Country Feedback).
NB: Also available on laser-disc.

BOOKS

☐ **"Book Of Songwords"**
anonymous, A5 booklet. (European)
R.E.M.'s lyrics as interpreted/guessed by the anonymous author.

☐ **"Another Book Of Songwords"**
anonymous, A5 booket. (European)
Lyrics to more R.E.M. songs, from the same source as above.

☐ **"Document Vol.1"**
anonymous, A4, approx 200 pages. (European)
A hefty book of photocopies of articles on, and interviews with REM, from around the world - includes some non-English language publications.

☐ **"Athens GA 1982 - 1992"**
anonymous, A4, approx 400 pages. (European)
From the same source as "Document" and in the same style. Reputedly, only 12 copies of this telephone directory sized collection are in existence.

☐ **"Songbook"**
privately printed, A4, 52pp. (UK)
More lyrical interpretations.

☐ **"Scrapbook vol.1"**
privately printed, A4, 64pp. (UK)
An insubstantial collection of photocopies from easily obtainable publications.

☐ **"Sketchbook"**
privately printed, A5, 28pp. (UK)
rudimentary sketches of REM members which should have been left at the bottom of the school desk!

(the last three listed are all from the same source, and pretty scrappy they are too!)

☐ **"Remarks - The Story Of R.E.M."**
by Tony Fletcher; published by Omnibus Press. ISBN 0 7119 1813 9 (UK)
A glossy 128 page volume telling the story of the band in a linear fashion up until the release of the "Green" album. Excellent photographs. An updated version is reputedly in the pipeline.

☐ **"A Few Chords & A Cloud Of Dust"**
a private printing by Total Recall (UK)
48 page discography - complete up until mid-1990 - the forerunner to this much updated publication.

☐ **"An REM Companion - It Crawled From the South"**
by Marcus Gray; published by Guinness. ISBN 0 85112 584 0. (UK)
A whopping 350 page tome first published in the spring of 1992. While not as pleasing visually as "Remarks", Marcus' book contains a staggering amount of information and informed comment about the band. Practically everything you could ever want to know about the life and times of R.E.M. is included here somewhere. Strangely, for such a comprehensive work, there are no discographies as such.

The following official tour books have been produced, and were available at concerts or from the R.E.M. fan club:

- ☐ Reconstruction Tour 1985
- ☐ Pageantry Tour 1986
- ☐ Work Tour 1987.
- ☐ Green World Tour 1989 - Part One: The East
- ☐ Green World Tour 1989 - Part Two: North America
- ☐ Green World Tour 1989 - Part Three: Europe
- ☐ Green World Tour 1989 - Part Four: North America

MEMORABILIA

- ☐ Promo only shoulder bag for "Fables of The Reconstruction".
- ☐ "Meadow In A Can" - a small round tin of seeds to promote the "Orange Crush" single.
- ☐ Small green plastic compass used to promote the "Stand" single.
- ☐ Promo only notepad (commonly known as a 'prayer book') with black & gold cover for "Losing My Religion".
- ☐ Promo only pillow-case for "Out Of Time".
- ☐ Promo coffee mug for 'Out Of Time'.
- ☐ "Out Of Time" suede tour jacket.

NOTE: Some of these promos may NOT be genuine - be warned!